Harmony at the Piano

Harmony at the Piano adapts the traditional study of keyboard harmony to the practical needs of modern piano students, using innovative exercises to help students practice their repertoire more deliberately, consciously, and creatively.

The author introduces the essential elements of harmony through extensive examples from real piano music. Rooted in the understanding that the language of tonal harmony is best assimilated at the keyboard, this textbook:

- Gives students effective practice methods for learning repertoire, including techniques for memorizing music in a deliberate, analytical way.
- Connects harmony to musical expression, enabling students to make interpretive decisions based on their understanding of harmony.
- Contains extensive practice drills in each chapter, including chord progressions, figured bass, melody harmonization, reduction techniques, transposition, repertoire study, and more.

Designed to support a full college or conservatory course in keyboard harmony, this book clearly connects the study of harmony to practical musicianship and keyboard skills, providing an essential resource for all instructors and students of advanced piano music.

Extensive online resources complement this textbook, including suggested realizations of the figured bass exercises and the original scores of the melody harmonization and fill-in-the-blank exercises, as well as additional exercises and examples.

Ken Johansen is Associate Professor of Keyboard Studies at the Peabody Institute of The Johns Hopkins University, where he has taught since 2002. He is a co-inventor of the piano sight-reading app *Read Ahead*, and the creator of *From the Ground Up*, a series of study editions published on *Practising the Piano Online Academy*. He holds degrees in piano performance from Peabody and the University of North Texas, and studied harmony and musicianship in Paris with Narcis Bonet.

Harmony at the Piano
Using Keyboard Harmony to Learn Advanced Piano Music

Ken Johansen

NEW YORK AND LONDON

Designed cover image: Giuliano Gargiulo

First published 2024
by Routledge
605 Third Avenue, New York, NY 10158

and by Routledge
4 Park Square, Milton Park, Abingdon, Oxon, OX14 4RN

Routledge is an imprint of the Taylor & Francis Group, an informa business

© 2024 Ken Johansen

The right of Ken Johansen to be identified as author of this work has been asserted in accordance with sections 77 and 78 of the Copyright, Designs and Patents Act 1988.

All rights reserved. No part of this book may be reprinted or reproduced or utilised in any form or by any electronic, mechanical, or other means, now known or hereafter invented, including photocopying and recording, or in any information storage or retrieval system, without permission in writing from the publishers.

Trademark notice: Product or corporate names may be trademarks or registered trademarks, and are used only for identification and explanation without intent to infringe.

Library of Congress Cataloging-in-Publication Data
Names: Johansen, Ken, author.
Title: Harmony at the piano / Ken Johansen.
Description: New York : Routledge, 2023. | Includes index.
Identifiers: LCCN 2023018627 (print) | LCCN 2023018628 (ebook) | ISBN 9781032366913 (hardback) | ISBN 9781032366890 (paperback) | ISBN 9781003333289 (ebook)
Subjects: LCSH: Piano--Instruction and study. | Harmonic analysis (Music) | Harmony.
Classification: LCC MT224 .J615 2023 (print) | LCC MT224 (ebook) | DDC 786.2125--dc23/eng/20230705
LC record available at https://lccn.loc.gov/2023018627
LC ebook record available at https://lccn.loc.gov/2023018628

ISBN: 978-1-032-36691-3 (hbk)
ISBN: 978-1-032-36689-0 (pbk)
ISBN: 978-1-003-33328-9 (ebk)

DOI: 10.4324/9781003333289

Typeset in Sabon
by Deanta Global Publishing Services, Chennai, India

Access the Support Material: www.routledge.com/9781032366890

In memory of Alain Naudé,

who made everything possible.

Contents

Introduction	1
1 Root Position Triads	4
2 First Inversion Triads	20
3 Sequences with Triads	35
4 Embellishing Tones	46
5 Second Inversion Triads	60
6 The Dominant Seventh Chord in Root Position	72
7 Inversions of the Dominant Seventh Chord	80
8 Secondary Dominant Chords	93
9 Diatonic Modulation	108
10 The Supertonic Seventh Chord	121
11 Sequences with Seventh Chords	136
12 The Leading Tone Seventh Chord in Minor	152
13 Secondary Diminished Chords	162
14 The Leading Tone Seventh Chord in Major	174
15 The Neapolitan Sixth Chord	182
16 Augmented Sixth Chords	191
17 Chromatic Voice Leading Techniques	204
Index	219

Introduction

Harmony at the Piano is a keyboard harmony textbook for piano students at conservatories and university music departments. While there are many textbooks available for the keyboard classes most undergraduate non-piano majors are required to take, this is to my knowledge the first textbook designed specifically for piano majors. Moreover, it is the first book to methodically connect the time-honored skills of keyboard harmony—figured bass, melody harmonization, and transposition—to the study of advanced piano repertoire. Nearly all the examples and exercises in this book are drawn from actual piano music, with the express goal of helping students to practice, interpret, and memorize their repertoire in a more conscious and effective way.

As anyone who studies advanced piano music knows, practicing in a conscious and effective way is a complex and demanding task. It requires an attentive ear, an analytical mind, an excellent memory, great physical coordination, and a creative approach to solving problems, not to mention patience, determination, and a host of other human qualities. To address all these facets of complete musicianship, musical education usually takes a divide-and-conquer approach, offering separate courses in sight-singing and ear training, written theory and analysis, and history and musicology, all intended to inform and support the students' work with their instrumental teachers. Unfortunately, this compartmentalized curriculum leaves to the individual students the difficult task of connecting all these elements of musicianship to their instrumental practice. It is not surprising then that many of them think their course work is unhelpful or irrelevant to their work in the practice room. This is a great shame, because these subjects—ear training, music theory, and analysis in particular—are indispensable for learning and interpreting music in a meaningful way.

Keyboard harmony is in many regards an ideal method of combining all these various facets of musicianship together in one activity. It brings music theory to the keyboard, helping students to assimilate harmonic patterns in a way that is at once physical, aural, and mental. It makes analysis a practical tool for learning and understanding the music we play. It trains the ear to hear inwardly what we see on the page. And above all, when applied to actual piano music, it gives pianists a powerful set of tools for practicing, interpreting, and memorizing their repertoire.

Pianists generally know how to practice the piano—slowly, hands separately, in small sections, and so on. What's more difficult is knowing how to practice the *music*. How do we actually learn a new piece of music—not just its notes and rhythms, but its patterns and structures? How do we recognize its innovations and eccentricities—the details that make it unique and beautiful? How do we decide how it should sound? How do we memorize it? *Harmony at the Piano* gives students the tools to answer these questions for themselves.

How This Book Is Organized

This book, like most harmony books, is organized by chord types, starting with triads and progressing through the various seventh chords and chromatic techniques, pausing along the way to take in sequences, embellishing tones, and modulation. This arrangement makes it possible to establish a firm foundation using the simplest chords, then to add progressively all the variations and subtleties of the more complex chords. More importantly, it allows different kinds of exercises and practice methods to be introduced gradually, contributing to the students' steady growth in skill and perception.

Each chapter is organized in roughly the same way—a musical example sets the scene, general theoretical principles are succinctly stated, preliminary drills and chord progressions develop basic skills, more complex exercises put these skills to practical use, and abundant musical examples provide material for analysis, transposition, memorization, and interpretation. To encourage independent thinking and to allow for different interpretations, the written commentary has been kept to a minimum. This is more a book to be played from than read.

The book contains many innovative exercises, including the following:

- **Chord Progressions:** Essential harmonic vocabulary using templates and ways of thinking that make it easy to transpose to all keys and chord positions.
- **Figured Bass:** A core component of keyboard harmony textbooks, here applied to actual piano repertoire, helping students to think from the bass upward.
- **Melody Harmonization:** Another key element of keyboard harmony books, but once again using real piano music, with annotations to help students hear the implied harmony.
- **Reductions:** Reducing complex textures to basic chords or simple outlines allows students to hear the fundamental lines and structures, and is an invaluable aid to memorizing and phrasing.
- **Reconstructions:** Melodic outlines and figured basses from which students reconstruct complete musical examples, leading to rapid and secure memorization.
- **Transposition:** Templates and practice methods for transposing musical excerpts to different keys using analysis and pattern identification.
- **Fill-in-the-Blank Exercises:** Excerpts from the piano literature with parts removed, which students learn to fill in by understanding the patterns.
- **Repertoire Study:** Extended excerpts for practicing, interpreting, and memorizing, using analysis, pattern recognition, harmonic reduction, and other practical tools.

How to Use This Book

Harmony at the Piano can be used as the core textbook in a keyboard harmony class for pianists, or as a supplementary text for courses that include a variety of keyboard skills. If it is used as a core text, most of its contents can be covered in two semesters, assuming a couple of hours of class time per week. As a supplementary text, it can serve as a resource of exercises and examples for different kinds of classes. Music theory teachers may wish to mine the book for its large collection of musical examples. Keyboard skills teachers will find ample material for their classes in the book's chord progressions, sequences, and figured bass exercises. Piano teachers will probably be most interested in the book's practice methods and pedagogical approaches to learning, interpreting, and memorizing piano music.

This book assumes a prior knowledge of the fundamental principles of tonal harmony, including Roman numeral analysis, figured bass numbers, and the basic rules of voice leading. It is therefore best used in the sophomore or junior year of an undergraduate program, after students have already taken two or three semesters of written music theory classes. This should not be seen as a redundant repetition of material already covered. Studying harmony at the keyboard is quite a different experience from writing it on paper; each approach benefits the other, and together they lead to a more complete mastery of the harmonic language.

Harmony at the Piano is intended for piano students studying the repertoire that normally figures on undergraduate juries and recitals: Bach suites and preludes and fugues, Classical sonatas from Haydn to Schubert, and Romantic character pieces from Chopin to Rachmaninoff. The book concentrates on the common harmonic language these composers share, rather than on trying to define their individual styles. Addressing such issues would swell the book to an enormous size, and deprive students of discovering these characteristics for themselves. Similarly, the book focuses on the inherent expressive qualities of harmony—tension and release, rhythmic movement, cadence feeling, and much more—rather than on performance practice issues such as ornamentation and historical performance styles, which are already the subject of a vast scholarly literature. Finally, there was regrettably not room to address improvisation in this volume, though its exercises lay a good foundation for future study in this important skill.

About the Online Support Material

This textbook includes extensive Online Support Material, including suggested realizations of the figured bass exercises and the original scores of the melody harmonizations and fill-in-the-blank exercises, as well as additional exercises and examples, which may be used for supplementary study, or for tests. Instructors may access this material at www.routledge.com/9781032366890.

1 Root Position Triads

We begin with the most fundamental chords, root position triads—three-note chords in which the root is in the bass. Passages made up entirely, or even primarily, of root position triads are rare in music after the Renaissance, but it is essential to learn how to connect these simple chords before we introduce their inversions.

1.1 Liszt: *Pater noster, Harmonies poétiques et religieuses,* **No. 5, 1–21**

Nearly all the chords in this piece, a transcription of Liszt's own choral setting of the Lord's Prayer, are root position triads. This restricted harmonic palette evokes an earlier era, and creates a solemn, somewhat austere sound.

PRELIMINARY EXERCISES

1.2 Chord Position and Style

Root position triads are said to be in octave, third, or fifth position, depending on which note of the chord is in the top voice, or soprano (**a.**). Harmony is usually studied in four voices (although keyboard music rarely adheres strictly to this model), which can be arranged in keyboard, chorale, or melody and accompaniment style (**b.**). We will begin with keyboard style and gradually introduce the other styles. Normally, the root of the chord is doubled.

1.3 Chord Shape Exercises

In the exercises below, add the two missing inner notes on each melodic note in the right hand, as shown in the first measure of the first exercise. A sharp below a bass note indicates that the third above the bass is raised a half step.

6 *Root Position Triads*

GENERAL PRINCIPLES: COMMON TONES AND CONTRARY MOTION

1.4 Three Rules of Voice Leading

Voice leading—the horizontal connection of chords—is governed by two broad principles: when two chords share a common tone, that tone is generally kept in the same voice; when there are no common tones, the upper voices usually move in contrary motion to the bass. These principles generate three simple rules for achieving good voice leading in root position triads.

1. When the bass moves by the interval of a fourth or a fifth, there is one common tone. Keep it in the same voice (**a.**).
2. When the bass moves by the interval of a third, there are two common tones. Keep them in the same voices (**b.**).
3. When the bass moves by step, there are no common tones. Move the other three voices in contrary motion to the bass (**c.**).

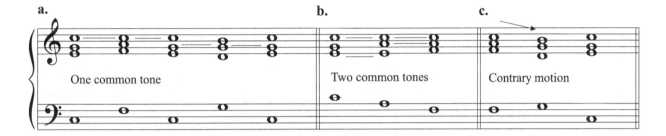

1.5 Schubert: Piano Sonata in A Minor, D. 845, I, 26–33

This example illustrates both the common tone principle (when the bass moves by a fourth) and the contrary motion principle (when the bass moves by step).

1.6 Schubert: Piano Sonata in B♭, D. 960, IV, 396–404

In this remarkable passage, the bass line moves entirely in thirds for six measures before descending stepwise to the cadence. Block the right hand in solid chords to better feel the two common tones between each chord and the next.

1.7 Chord Progression with Three Kinds of Bass Motion

The following progression (I–vi–IV–V–I) contains bass motion by seconds, thirds, and fourths, so it is ideal for learning how to connect root position triads following the three rules of voice leading. It is written in such a way that it can be played in all 24 keys, using all three right-hand positions in alternation. The first four keys are written out below. Continue with the same pattern using the table of 24 keys in **1.8** to guide you through the remaining keys and positions. If you have any difficulty transposing this progression, try playing the bass line by itself first.

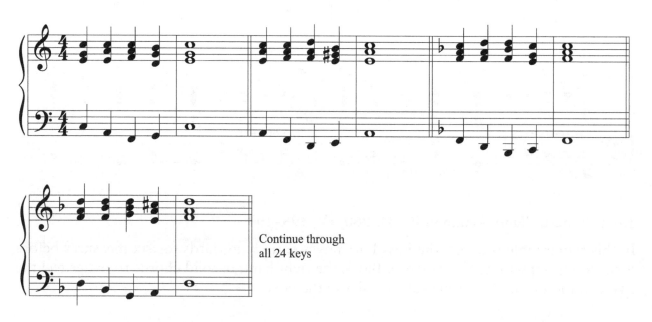

Continue through all 24 keys

As you play this progression (and all the progressions to come), strive to make it not only accurate, but pleasing to the ear. Use the pedal to connect the chords to each other, listen for the simultaneous sounding of all four notes of each chord, bring out the soprano while also listening to the bass line, and above all, try to avoid playing each chord with the same intensity. Harmonic inflection is guided by the principle of tension and release—tension increases as we move through the subdominant (IV or ii) toward the dominant (V) and decreases as the dominant resolves to the tonic (I).

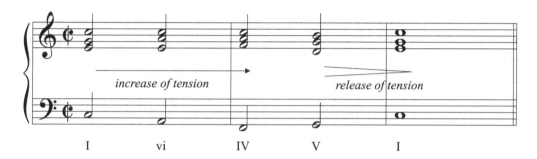

1.8 Table of 24 Keys

This table moves counterclockwise through the circle of fifths, interspersing each major key with its relative minor. The chords are alternatingly in octave, third, and fifth positions, and serve as starting points for the progression in 1.7.

1.9 Figured Basses Following the Three Rules

In figured bass, the keyboard player plays a given bass line with the left hand and adds chords in the right hand following figures added below (or sometimes above) the bass line. The letter above the first note indicates the starting position for the soprano. If you follow the three rules of voice leading correctly, the last chord in each exercise should be in octave position.

1.10 Tchaikovsky Reconstruction

Reconstruct the missing right hand in this piano piece by following the three rules in **1.4**. The rhythm of the right hand is the same as the left hand.

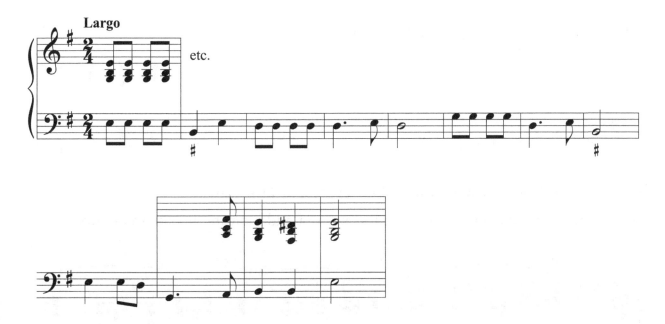

EXCEPTION TO THE COMMON TONE PRINCIPLE

1.11 Transferred Common Tone

To create more interesting melodic lines, composers often make exceptions to the principle of keeping common tones between chords in the same voices. Instead, they transfer the common tone to another voice, or to another octave, usually resulting in contrary motion between the bass and the upper voices. This example shows two progressions in which this exception is commonly used. The dotted lines show the transference of a common tone to a different voice, and the arrows show the resulting contrary motion between the bass and the upper voices.

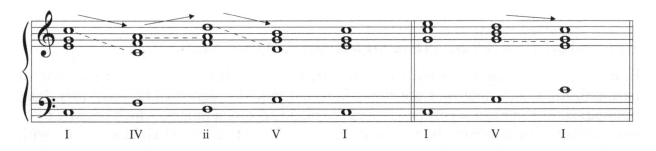

1.12 Chopin: Nocturne in G Minor, Op. 37, No. 1, 41–44

In this passage, Chopin uses two transferred common tones to create a melodic line that arches gracefully to a peak in the third measure.

1.13 Chopin: Nocturne in G Minor, Op. 15, No. 3, 113–120

Find the transferred common tones in this excerpt and indicate them with arrows.

1.14 Brahms: *Ich schell mein Horn ins Jammertal*, Op. 43, No. 3

In this song, a setting of an old German text, Brahms deliberately uses an old style of harmonization, including root position triads and modal cadences. The voice part (here omitted) is the same as the soprano line of the piano accompaniment, which because of its low register is written entirely on one staff. Indicate the transferred common tones with arrows.

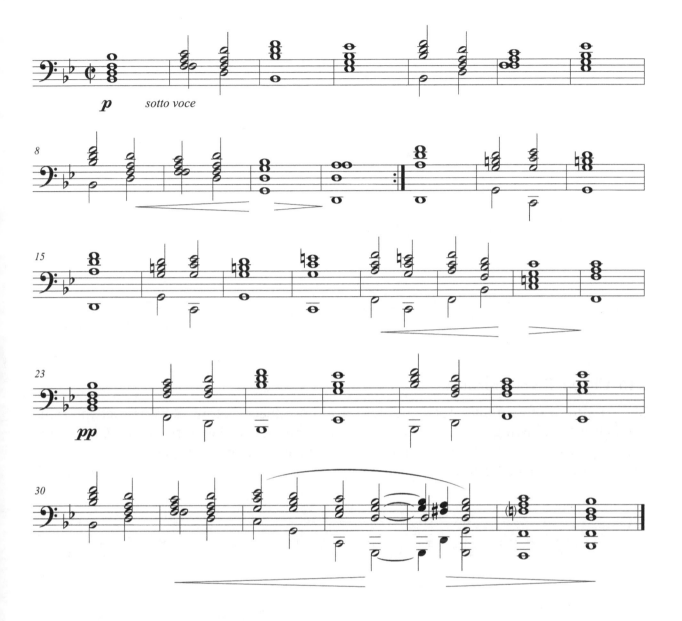

1.15 Handel: Lessons for Princess Anne, Nos. 1, 2, and 4

In these three figured bass exercises, a strict adherence to the rule of keeping common tones in the same voice would produce very repetitive soprano lines (try it for yourself to verify this). Transferring some of the common tones to another voice will help to alleviate this problem. Simply use the suggested starting position, then follow the arrows to move one position higher or lower than you normally would. These are only suggested solutions, however. Try different starting positions and use transferred common tones in various places to come up with your own solutions.

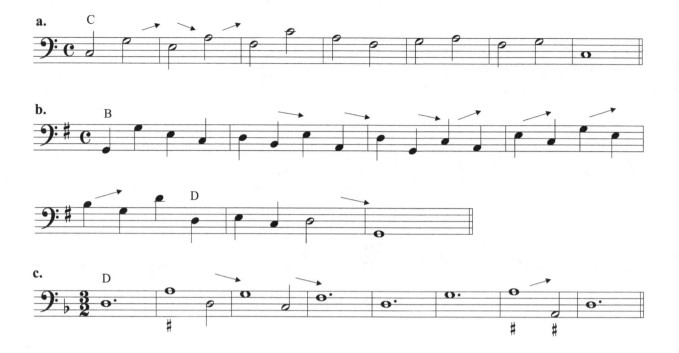

1.16 Chopin Reconstructions

The bass lines of examples **1.12** and **1.13** are reproduced below. Reconstruct the right-hand chords following the three rules in **1.4** and the indications in the score. Check your accuracy by referring back to the examples, then memorize the passages using your understanding of the voice leading.

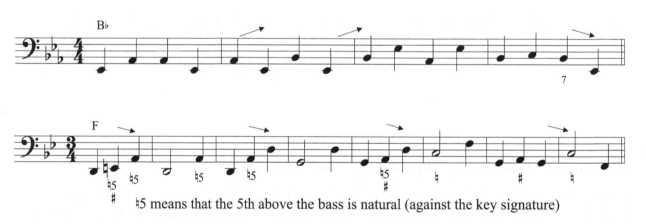

♮5 means that the 5th above the bass is natural (against the key signature)

1.17 Brahms Reconstruction

This song is similar to the one in example **1.14**. Reconstruct the right hand of the accompaniment following the three rules in **1.4** and the indications in the score. "No 3rd" means leave out the third of the chord (play the root and fifth only, as in measure 11 of example **1.14**).

EXCEPTION TO THE CONTRARY MOTION PRINCIPLE

1.18 Cadences

Cadences punctuate the ends of musical phrases with varying degrees of conclusiveness. Below, the five types of cadences are given in their simplest form, to which we will gradually add other forms.

- **Perfect Authentic Cadence (PAC):** V resolves to I with both chords in root position, and the root in the soprano on I. The most conclusive kind of cadence, equivalent to a period in punctuation.
- **Imperfect Authentic Cadence (IAC):** Includes all the other forms of resolution from V to I, in this case with the third of the chord in the soprano on I. Equivalent to a semicolon.

16 Root Position Triads

- **Deceptive Cadence (DC):** V resolves unexpectedly to vi instead of I, like a question mark.
- **Half Cadence (HC):** The phrase ends on V, creating a need for continuation, like a dash or comma.
- **Plagal Cadence (PC):** IV to I, as in the final "Amen" at the end of a hymn.

Play these five cadences, giving each of them an inflection appropriate to their punctuation. To read them in minor, simply imagine the key signature of C minor, retaining the B♮s for the leading tone.

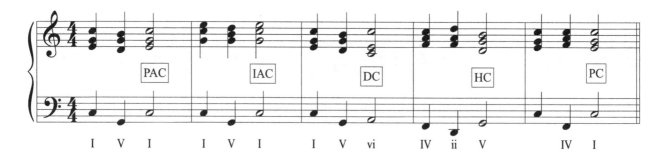

1.19 The Deceptive Cadence

Normally, when the bass moves by step, the upper voices all move in contrary motion. In the deceptive cadence, however, the leading tone must rise when it is in the soprano to avoid being "frustrated," that is, deprived of its natural tendency to resolve upward. This creates an exceptional doubling of the third on vi, which is felt as an octave shape in the pianist's hand (**a.**). The need for this upward resolution is felt even more acutely in minor, where the downward motion of the leading tone would produce an augmented second (**b.**).

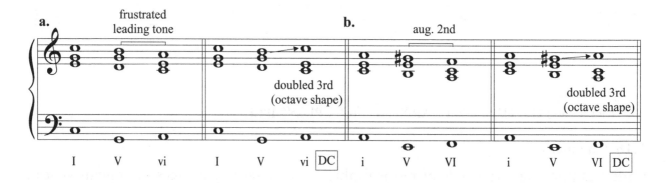

1.20 Progressions with Deceptive Cadences

Practice the following progressions to ingrain the new shapes and voice leading of the deceptive cadence. Progressions **a.** and **b.** illustrate two ways to continue from vi to IV, using either the "high road" to continue to an IAC, or the "low road" to lead to a PAC. In minor, the leading tone must resolve upwards in all three positions of the DC to avoid augmented seconds (**c.**). This produces two-note resolutions in the first two positions (actually, the A is doubled at the unison). Remember to follow the movement of harmonic tension and release as you play these progressions. Transpose to several other keys.

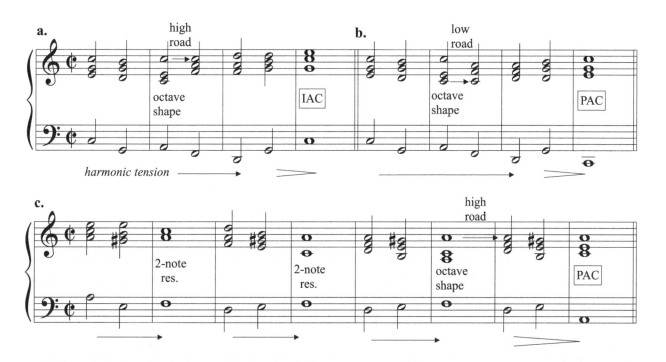

1.21 Figured Basses with Deceptive Cadences

In these exercises, find the deceptive cadences and resolve them as in **1.20**. When the vi chord has the octave shape, choose either the "high road" or the "low road" afterwards, so that you end with a PAC. The solution for the first exercise is given as a model. Starting positions are suggested, but it is always beneficial to try other positions as well.

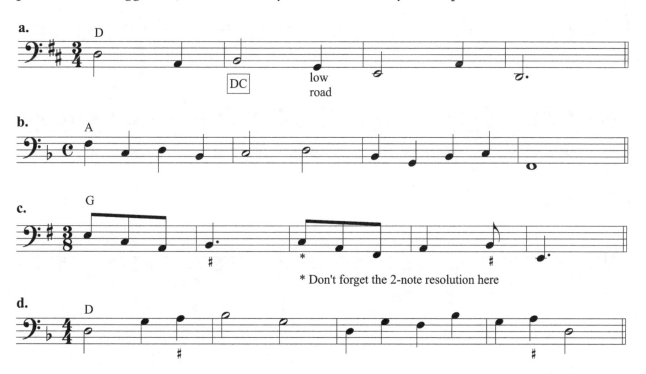

* Don't forget the 2-note resolution here

18 *Root Position Triads*

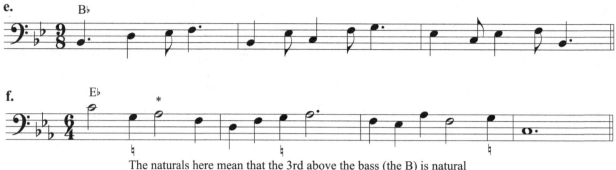

The naturals here mean that the 3rd above the bass (the B) is natural

1.22 Schubert Reconstruction

Reconstruct the right hand of this song accompaniment following all the rules and exceptions you have learned in this chapter. The ♮5 means that the fifth above the bass (the B) is natural. *Etwas langsam* means "rather slow."

2 First Inversion Triads

Using first inversion triads—triads with the third of the chord in the bass—composers have the possibility of writing smoother, less disjunct bass lines than root position triads alone can produce. This melodic bass line forms an important counterpoint with the melody in the upper voice. In this chapter, we study this relationship between the outer voices and begin to learn the essentials of figured bass accompaniment.

2.1 Beethoven: Piano Concerto No. 4, Op. 58, I, 1–14

The beautiful opening of this concerto illustrates well the counterpoint between the bass and the melody that first inversion chords help to make possible. Play the outer voices by themselves to better hear their relationship to each other.

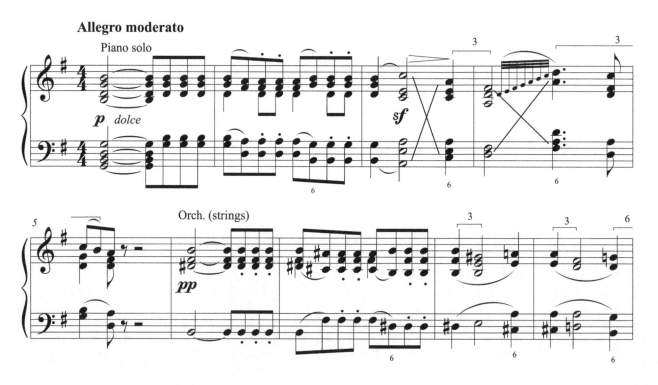

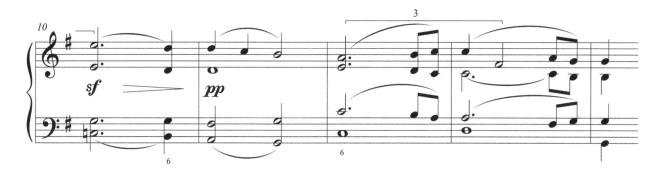

In this excerpt, we can already observe several patterns in the relationship between the outer voices:

- Out of eight first inversion triads (indicated by the figured bass number 6 under the staff), all but two of them have the root of the chord in the soprano, creating an interval of a sixth between the outer voices.
- When the bass of a first inversion triad moves up a step to a root position triad, the outer voice usually descends by the interval of a third (marked with a 3 over a bracket). Sometimes this pattern has intervening figuration (measures 4–5 and 12–13), and once the descending third is inverted to an ascending sixth (measures 9–10), but the idea is the same.
- In measures 3–4, the outer voices exchange notes, prolonging the same harmony by a change of inversion (indicated by Xs).

RELATIONSHIPS BETWEEN THE OUTER VOICES

2.2 Three Common Patterns

In first inversion triads, the root is most often in the soprano, creating an interval of a sixth between the outer voices.

In addition, there are three common patterns between the outer voices involving first inversion triads:

a. **Falling Third:** When the bass moves up a step from a first inversion triad to a root position triad, the soprano frequently falls a third (from the root of the first chord to the third of the second chord).
b. **Parallel Sixths:** When there are two or more first inversion chords in a row, the soprano almost always moves in parallel sixths with the bass.
c. **Voice Exchange:** When the bass moves from root position to first inversion of the same chord (or *vice versa*), the soprano often exchanges notes with the bass (indicated by Xs).

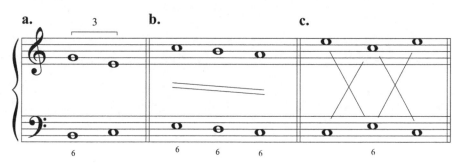

2.3 Making an Outer Voice Reduction (Haydn: Piano Sonata in A♭, Hob. XVI:46, I, 1–3)

Finding these patterns often requires reducing one or both of the outer voices to their essential notes. The highly ornamented melody in the Haydn phrase below, for example, conceals both a falling third pattern and parallel sixths with the bass. Reducing such passages to their essential outlines reveals the basic simplicity of the structure, making them easier to learn and memorize, and helping us to hear the longer line.

To make an outer voice reduction, follow these two steps:

1. Reduce the bass line first, removing octave leaps, repeated notes, arpeggios, and ornamental notes. If there are rests, move the notes back to the nearest beat, as in the Haydn above.
2. For each reduced bass note, choose one main note of the melody to go with it. Normally, this note will form a consonant interval with the bass (a third, sixth, fifth, or octave). Two-note slurs such as those in the Haydn often indicate that the first note is dissonant, and the second note is the chord tone.

In the examples that follow (**2.4–2.8**), play each excerpt first, then play (or write down) an outer voice reduction. Write a 6 underneath the first inversion triads and indicate any of the three common patterns you find with the markings used in the examples above.

2.4 Haydn: Piano Sonata in C, Hob. XVI:35, III, 1–25

2.5 Mozart: Piano Sonata in B♭, K. 281, III, 1–8

Remember that, in two-note slurs, it is usually the second note that is the chord tone. In measure 3, the two first inversion triads have, exceptionally, the fifth of the chord in the soprano rather than the root, producing parallel tenths with the bass, rather than sixths.

24 *First Inversion Triads*

2.6 Mozart: Piano Sonata in A Minor, K. 310, III, 37–51

2.7 Beethoven: Piano Sonata in D, Op. 28, II, 17–22

2.8 Schumann: *Nordisches Lied* ("Nordic Song"), Album for the Young, Op. 68, No. 40, 1–8

This example does not require a reduction, but it contains all three outer voice patterns, some of which are partially hidden. Note the exceptional voicing of the first inversion chord in measures 3 and 7. *Im Volkston* means "in folk style."

2.9 Melodic Reconstructions

The melodies of the preceding five examples are given below in reduction, together with the symbols indicating our three outer voice relationships. You can use these reductions to check your own solutions, but more importantly, they can help you to memorize these passages in a deliberate, analytical way. Reconstructing the bass lines from these annotated melodies helps us to relate the two hands to each other. Reducing the melodies to their main notes helps us to knit the phrases together in long lines, and to hear which notes are ornamental and which ones are fundamental. Practice each excerpt in the following ways:

1. Reconstruct the bass line from the melody. This should give you the reduction you made directly from the score previously.
2. Add what you can remember of the rest of the right hand. Go back to the original to check any passages you are unsure of. If you like, add further annotations to the reduction to help remind you of these details.
3. Add what you can remember of the rest of the left hand, including the inner notes. Again, go back to the original in cases of doubt and add further notes to help jog your memory.
4. Try the excerpt entirely from memory.

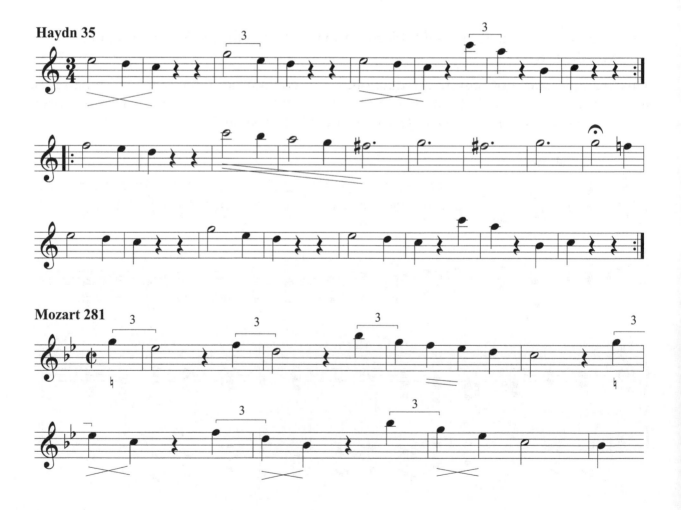

FIGURED BASS WITH FIRST INVERSION TRIADS

2.10 Doubling and Three Basic Chord Shapes

So far in this chapter, we have only been concerned with the outer voices. Now, as we begin to add the middle voices, we will be confronted with the question of doubling. In three-voice textures such as we have seen in several of the preceding examples, we simply add the missing note of the chord in the middle voice (**a.**, below). In four voices, the root, third, or fifth may be doubled depending on the function of the chord (see **2.11**). These doublings produce, respectively, an octave shape in the right hand (**b.**), a sixth shape (**c.**), or a fourth (**d.**). There are other possibilities (**e.** and **f.**), but they are less common so we will not study them here.

28 First Inversion Triads

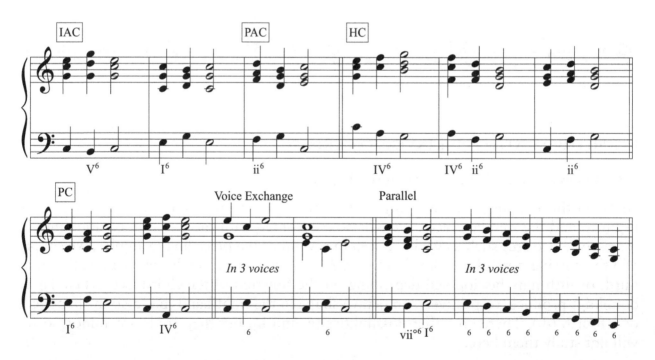

2.11 Cadences and Other Common Patterns

Using first inversion triads, we can expand our vocabulary of cadences. The cadences and other patterns below are not a complete catalog of all the possibilities, only a selection of the most common ones. As you play them, notice the different chord shapes for the first inversion triads:

- **Octave Shape:** Used for I⁶, V⁶, and IV⁶ (when it goes to I).
- **Sixth Shape:** Used for ii⁶ and vii°⁶.
- **Fourth Shape:** Used on IV⁶ (when it goes to V) and when playing in three voices.

You can also play these cadences in the parallel minor by imagining the key signature of C minor, keeping the B♮s for the leading tone.

To transpose these cadences, try using the template below, which presents them in an abstract way that is not dependent on a particular key. Start by finding the bass line using the Roman numerals, then add the soprano line, indicated by the Arabic numeral scale degrees. Finally, add the middle voices, using the chord shapes (8ᵛᵉ, 6th, or 4th) to remind you of the doublings.

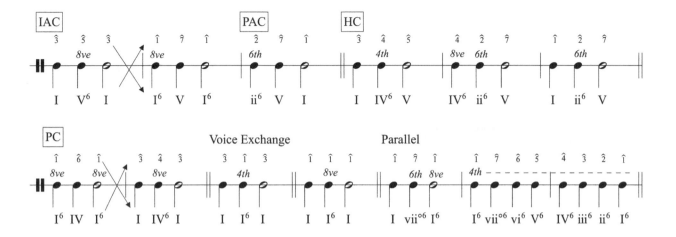

2.12 Short Figured Basses

The following exercises are made up of various combinations of the cadences and patterns in **2.11**. Whenever there is a 6, put the root (the sixth above the bass) in the soprano, then find the remaining notes of the soprano using the three outer voice patterns (**2.2**). Fill in the middle voices following the doublings in **2.11**.

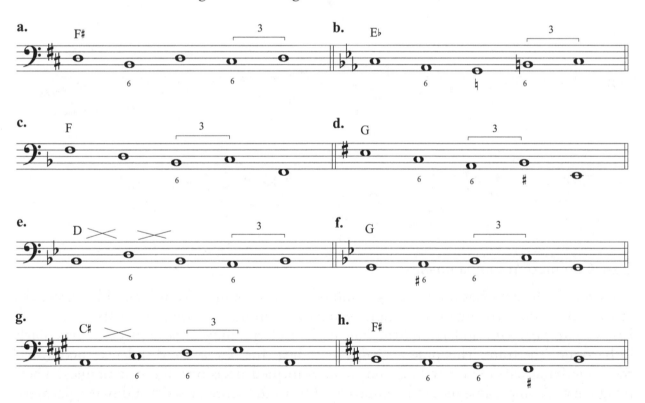

2.13 Handel: Lessons for Princess Anne, Nos. 7–9

These figured basses are a bit more florid, containing arpeggiations of the same chord (root position and first inversion—make a voice exchange, usually with the inner voice) and passing tones (marked with a dash—just hold the preceding chord). Again, find the soprano first using the three outer voice patterns. Play parallel first inversion triads in three voices for a lighter texture.

2.14 Continuo Accompaniments

Continuo is the art of accompanying a soloist or an ensemble from figured bass, usually at the harpsichord or organ. For pianists, making continuo accompaniments is an excellent way to hear and understand the harmonic underpinning of solo pieces, particularly in Baroque repertoire. This practice helps us to hear the phrases and cadences better, feel the underlying harmonic rhythm, and make informed decisions about dynamics. These imaginary accompaniments can be improvised from the score or written down separately. Writing them down, as we will do in the next two examples, allows us to practice in several fruitful ways. We can:

1. Play the original while someone else plays the continuo on another piano.
2. Play the original while imagining the continuo.
3. Play the written continuo accompaniment while imagining and singing the original.

4. Play a continuo accompaniment from the original.
5. Play the original while looking at the written continuo (a useful memory test).

2.15 Bach: French Suite No. 2 in C Minor, Minuet, 1–8

This excerpt can serve as a model for making continuo reductions. The original score is in the upper staff, annotated with analysis of the outer voice patterns, while the lower staff shows the reduction, which reveals the cadences and phrase lengths (two four-measure phrases), faster harmonic rhythm leading into the cadences, and overall dynamic inflection. Play the original and the reduction in the five ways described in **2.14**.

2.16 Bach: French Suite No. 3 in B Minor, Minuet, 1–16

Analyze the outer voice relationships in the original (some of the patterns actually occur between the bass and the "middle" voice), then write your own continuo accompaniment. Once again, practice as suggested in **2.14**.

2.17 Leonardo Leo: Toccata in G Minor, 1–22

In this movement, a figured bass has been added to help you play a continuo accompaniment directly from the score. Start by playing a chord with each bass note, following the general outline of the upper staff, then make a more reduced version, playing a new chord only when the harmony changes and adjusting the right hand to keep the voice leading smooth.

34 *First Inversion Triads*

3 Sequences with Triads

Harmonic sequences play an important role in tonal music. The repetition of a pair of chords at a higher or lower pitch creates a sense of movement and direction, which only comes to rest at the cadence. In this chapter, we study the three most common types of sequences in their simplest diatonic forms, using root position and first inversion triads. In later chapters, we will add further variations to these basic patterns.

3.1 Bach: Prelude in B♭, *Well-Tempered Clavier*, Book 1, 1–6

The whole of this improvisatory prelude is made up of embellished sequences. This excerpt shows the first two. The sequential unit is indicated with a bracket. The first sequence has three units, each one a diatonic third lower than the previous one. This is therefore called a sequence of descending thirds. A short cadence takes us back to the tonic in measure 3, where a new sequence begins. This one has a longer unit of a whole measure, which is repeated a step higher in measure 4, and partially repeated another step higher in measure 5, before returning once again to the tonic. We call this a sequence of ascending seconds.

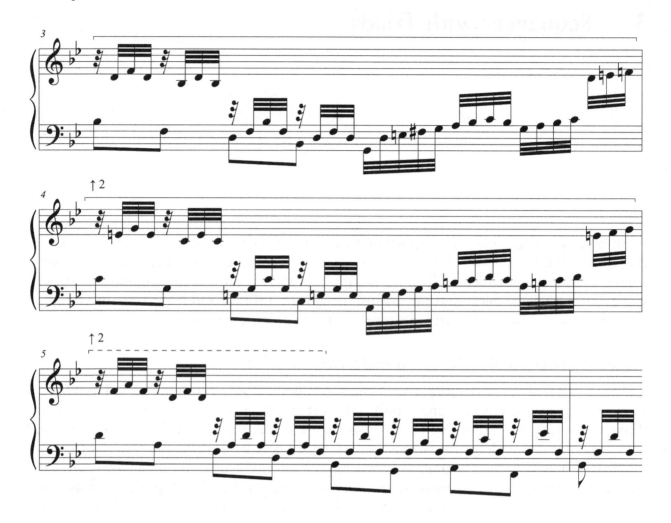

3.2 Performance Considerations

The mass of notes in this prelude can be reduced to just a handful of chords, as can be seen in the reduction below. Obviously, reducing a passage to a few simple chords makes it much easier to learn. It also allows us to hear the larger harmonic structure more easily, and to make decisions about dynamics. Playing this reduction, we clearly hear the octave descent from tonic to tonic of the first sequence, followed by the more energetic rising sequence to iii and the subsequent relaxation of the return to the tonic. In addition to this large-scale dynamic scheme, it is useful to ask ourselves which of the two chords within the sequential unit is more active, or energetic. In the first sequence, the second chord is shorter, but more active because of the leaps and contrary motion, which create momentum toward the next step of the sequence. In the rising sequence, the second chord is again more active than the first, because of its energetic ascending scales. Adding a plus sign (+), as in the reduction above, is a simple way of notating this harmonic inflection.

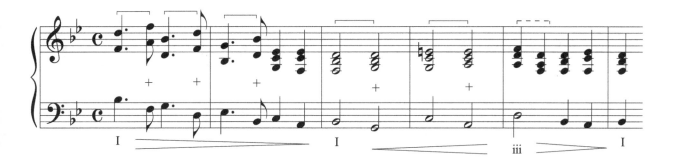

THE THREE TYPES OF SEQUENCES

3.3 Naming the Sequences

There are three main types of sequences, which we name according to the interval by which the unit moves. Other types of sequences are possible, but less common.

- **Descending Seconds:** The initial unit is usually I and IV, and is sequenced down by step (**a.**). This sequence is equally common in major and minor. It is often called "circle of fifths" because the roots of the chords descend by fifths.
- **Ascending Seconds:** The initial unit is again usually I and IV, but is sequenced up by step (**b.**). This sequence is usually in major.
- **Descending Thirds:** The initial unit is I and V, and is sequenced down by thirds (**c.**). This sequence is almost always in major.

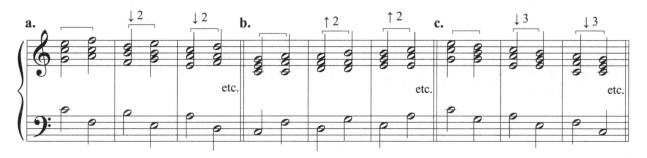

3.4 Descending Seconds

Below are two versions of the descending seconds sequence, the first (**a.**) using all root position triads, the second (**b.**) alternating root position with first inversion. Both are given first in major, then in minor. Memorize the patterns and practice them in all 24 keys, alternating the major key with its relative minor and proceeding counterclockwise around the circle of fifths (C major, A minor, F major, D minor, etc.).

38 *Sequences with Triads*

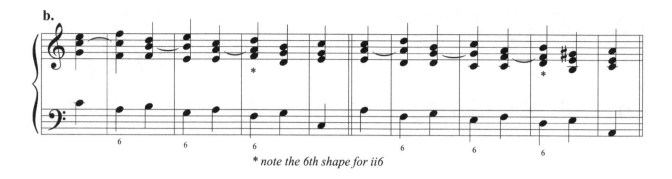

*note the 6th shape for ii6

3.5 Ascending Seconds

Below are four versions of the ascending seconds sequence, the first two (**a.** and **b.**) using all root position triads, the second two alternating first inversion and root position (**c.** and **d.**). Memorize the patterns and transpose them to other major keys.

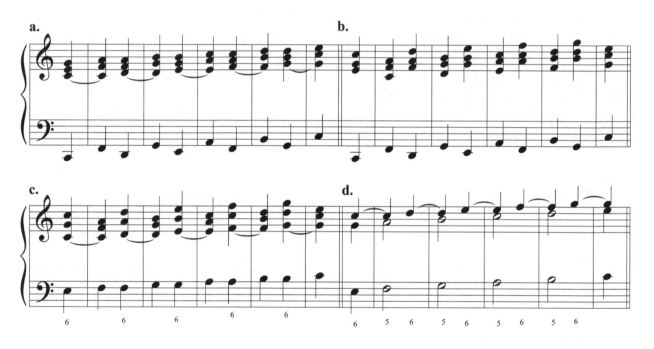

3.6 Descending Thirds

Below are two versions of the descending thirds sequence, the first (**a.**) using root position triads, the second (**b.**) alternating root position and first inversion. Memorize the patterns and transpose them to other major keys.

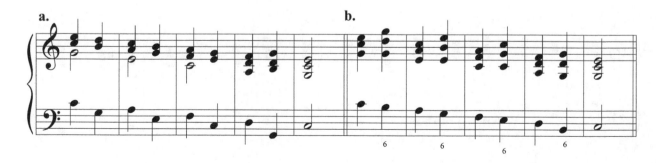

EXAMPLES

Play each of the examples below, then do the following:

- Play a reduction of some kind, as suggested for each example.
- Identify the type of sequence (which of the model sequences in **3.4–3.6** does it come closest to?) and put a bracket over each unit of the sequence (as in **3.1**).
- Notice any changes or variations from one step of the sequence to the next.
- Take note of the expressive melodic and rhythmic figuration that enlivens the sequence. In other words, what does the composer do to make the basic sequence unique and beautiful?
- Add dynamics to show the overall inflection of each sequence, then decide which of the two chords in the sequential unit is more active and put a plus sign (+) on it (as in **3.2**).

3.7 Bach: Little Prelude in D, BWV 925, 8–13

This excerpt contains all three types of sequences, the last of which uses seventh chords (see Chapter 11). Make a continuo accompaniment in quarter-note chords. In measures 10–11, the syncopations in the upper voice will need to be aligned with the beats.

3.8 Haydn: Piano Sonata in A, Hob. XVI:12, II, 25–38

To find the essential patterns, reduce the right hand to one note per measure (except measures 36–37) and the middle voice to one or two notes per measure. Also identify the three outer voice patterns from Chapter 2.

3.9 Haydn: Piano Sonata in A♭, Hob. XVI:46, I, 49–45

To start with, make a two-voice reduction in half notes (see **2.3**). From that, you can add chords in the right hand, as for a continuo accompaniment, or play the right hand as written with the left hand reduced (and *vice versa*).

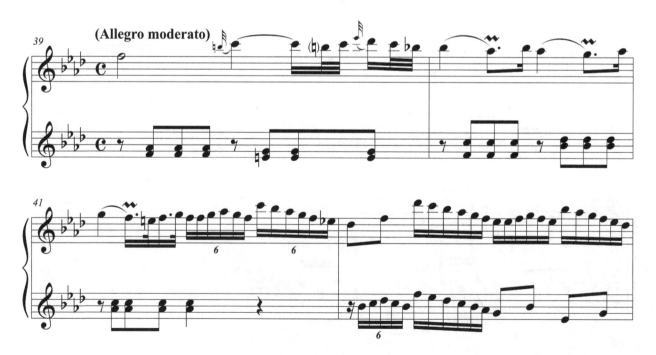

3.10 Beethoven: Piano Concerto No. 5, Op. 73, II, 20–26

Imagine an orchestral accompaniment to this passage in sustained, keyboard style harmony and accompany someone else playing the piano part.

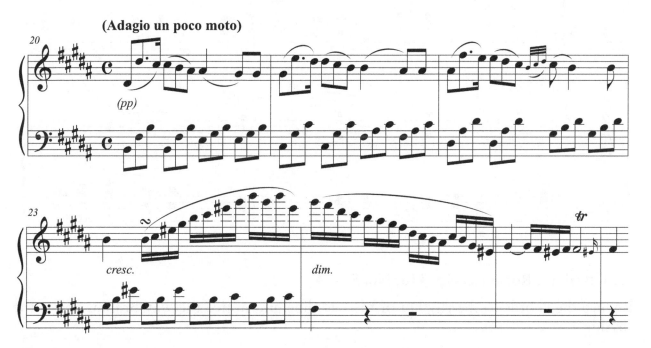

42 Sequences with Triads

3.11 Beethoven: Piano Sonata in E, Op. 109, I, 1–4

Reduce to simple blocked chords.

3.12 Schumann: Waltz, from *Albumblätter*, Op. 124, No. 4, 17–28

To find the basic form of the sequence, reduce the melody to its main notes (one note per measure) and play this against the bass line.

3.13 Brahms, Romanze, Op. 118, No. 5, 1–4

Reduce the chords to the rhythm of the bass line and notice the way Brahms varies the rhythm.

FILL-IN-THE-BLANK EXERCISES

In these passages, the initial sequential units are written out, but their repetitions are left blank. By following the patterns, with some help from the written instructions, you'll be able to reconstitute the missing notes. These exercises in reconstruction take longer to learn than reading the passages as written, but they force us to understand what we are playing, and help us to memorize in an analytical way.

3.14 Bach

Analyze each sequence pattern carefully before trying to play it. It helps to practice the left hand by itself first, then block the right hand into chords before playing it as written. To find out why Bach changes the left-hand pattern in measure 3, try continuing the pattern exactly and see what happens. Memorize the passage.

44 *Sequences with Triads*

3.15 Mozart

Piano concertos such as this one often contain sequential passages, especially in their transitional sections. Try first playing only the left hand in block chords, then add the right-hand scale passages. Note that, while the movement is in C major, this passage is in G major. Memorize the passage.

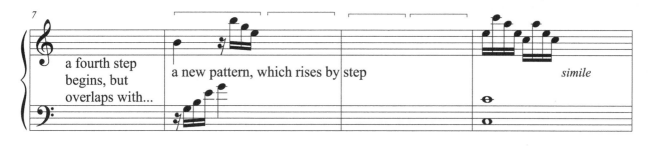

3.16 Chopin

Find the melody first, then add a single-note bass line, and finally the remaining details. Note the slight change to the left-hand pattern in measure 6 (compared to measure 2). Memorize the passage.

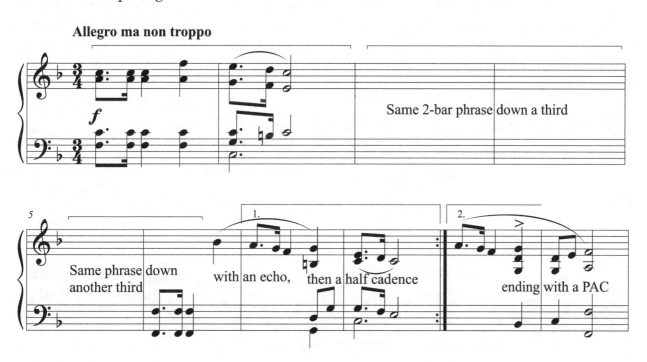

4 Embellishing Tones

Throughout this book, we practice reducing musical textures to their essential chords and outlines, removing the embellishing tones, or non-chord tones as they are also called. This helps us to uncover the fundamental harmonic progressions underneath the music's surface detail, but in doing so, we remove some of what is most beautiful and expressive. In the first part of this chapter, we consider the musical effect of these embellishing tones, and their importance in achieving an expressive musical performance. In the second part, we focus on suspensions and their realization in figured bass accompaniment.

4.1 Mozart: Piano Sonata in B♭, K. 333, I, 1–10

Labeling all the embellishing tones in this example looks rather ridiculous, but shows how vital these non-chord tones are to Mozart's melodic style. Play this passage as written first, enjoying the florid exuberance of the right-hand melody. Notice how some of these melodic dissonances—particularly those that fall on strong beats—call clear attention to themselves, while others—especially the running sixteenth notes—pass almost unnoticed.

DOI: 10.4324/9781003333289-5

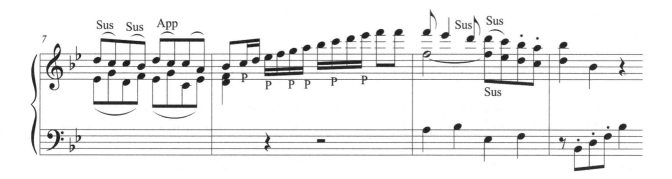

The best way to appreciate the beauty that embellishing tones bring to a passage is to remove them ("embellish" means to make more beautiful). When we play the plain, dull reduction below, we realize that Mozart's embellishing tones provide not only the tension and release of dissonance and resolution, but rhythmic variety, energy, and forward motion.

In the sections that follow, we look closely at the specific characteristics of the different embellishing tones, and propose three practice methods that help us to hear them better, so that we may fully respond to them in our playing.

GENERAL PRINCIPLES

4.2 Summary of Embellishing Tones

Embellishing tones go by many different names, but fall into two main categories: passing tones, which fill in a gap, normally of a third, with stepwise motion; and neighbor tones, which also move stepwise up or down, but return to their starting note. As shown in the

48 *Embellishing Tones*

chart below, which gives the names and abbreviations of the most common embellishing tones:

- **Passing Tones** can go up or down, and can be diatonic or chromatic, accented or unaccented.
- **Neighbor Tones** can likewise go up or down, and can be diatonic or chromatic, accented or unaccented. Combinations of upper and lower neighbor tones are called double neighbor tones.
- **Incomplete Neighbor Tones** are either approached by a leap (appoggiaturas), resolved by a leap (escape tones), or continue to the same note (anticipations).
- **Suspensions and Retardations** are also incomplete neighbor tones but are approached by the same pitch. They can be single or double, tied to the preceding note or repeated. Suspensions resolve downward whereas retardations resolve upward. We will study the different kinds of suspensions in detail later in this chapter.

Each of these dissonant embellishing tones is preceded by a consonant chord tone, called the preparation, and followed by the resolution, also a consonant chord tone. This three-step process in the treatment of dissonance has important ramifications for the performer.

Passing Tones (PT)

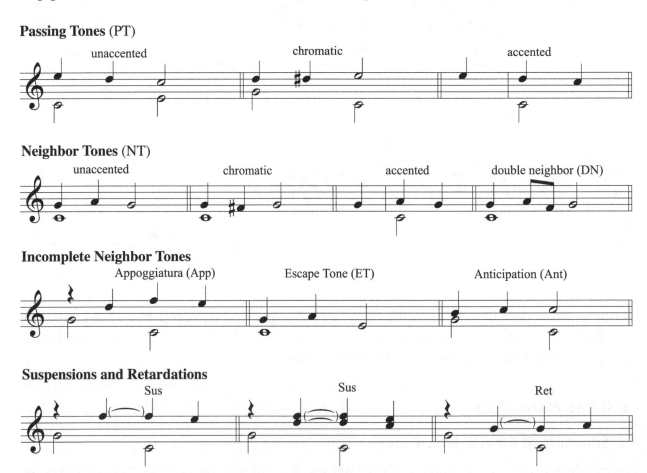

Neighbor Tones (NT)

Incomplete Neighbor Tones

Suspensions and Retardations

PERFORMANCE CONSIDERATIONS

4.3 Inflection of Embellishing Tones

Each of the different embellishing tones has its own expressive character. While the musical context plays a decisive role in determining this character, we can nevertheless make certain generalizations, as illustrated in the chart below.

- **Passing Tones** create a sense of flowing forward motion and connection. When they are unaccented (**a.**), they should lead forward to the next note. When they are accented, they can sometimes be slightly emphasized, especially in two-note slurs (**b.**).
- **Neighbor Tones** stand out from their surroundings because they are preceded and followed by the same note. It often helps to imagine a *crescendo* on the preparation note (**c.**). Escape tones have a more wistful quality because they strive upward only to fall back to a lower point (**d.**).
- **Anticipations** have a strong pull to the resolution note, especially when the preparation note is the leading tone. They should not be played too short, but given the length and time they need to be heard against the rest of the chord (**e.**).
- **Appoggiaturas** have a feeling of yearning because they reach beyond the goal note of the resolution (**f.**). Giving the preparation note as much, or even more, importance than the appoggiatura itself can help to avoid an isolated accent, especially when the dissonance is approached by a large interval.
- **Suspensions** are highly expressive because of the tension created by the delayed resolution. The preparation note is again very important, especially when it is syncopated and tied to the suspended note (**g.**). When the repeated note is not tied, the preparation note should be felt as an upbeat to the dissonant note (**h.** and **i.**).

4.4 Practice Methods

The natural decay of sound on the piano is one of the primary obstacles to hearing the expressive dissonance of embellishing tones. The following practice methods help to overcome this difficulty and respond musically to dissonances that can sometimes be difficult to hear.

50 *Embellishing Tones*

Repeat and React: In this practice method, we repeat notes that are fading so that we can hear them better and react to them musically. There are different applications of this technique, starting with repeating the accompanying chords (or single notes, as the case may be) against each note of the melody. This gives us an audible demonstration of the varying degrees of dissonance each melodic note has against the underlying harmony. For example, in the Mozart passage from **4.1**, we can block the left-hand accompaniment in solid chords to better hear the harmony. Do this slowly and softly while listening carefully to the effect of each melody note against the chord.

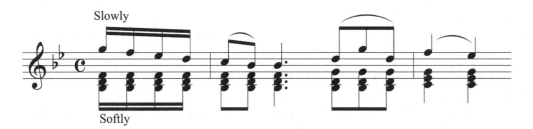

Sometimes it is the dissonant melodic notes that need repeating so that we may hear them better. This works especially well with suspensions. Measure 9 of the same Mozart passage contains both a single and a double suspension (marked below with asterisks) that are hard to hear, particularly in the relatively high register of the right hand. Repeating these tied notes and moving the right hand an octave lower makes these dissonances more audible.

Linger and Listen: In this practice method, we simply linger momentarily on the dissonance, especially on a longer note that is starting to decay, and listen closely to make sure we hear the dissonance against the other voice, or voices. In this Haydn example, we linger on the suspensions (marked with added fermatas here) to listen for the dissonance they form with the lower voice.

Prepare and Resolve: The three-step treatment of dissonance is fundamentally a rhythmic phenomenon: the preparation leads forward to the goal point—the dissonance—and the resolution recedes from that point. For the performer, following this ebb and flow of tension and release helps to create a natural sense of phrasing and rhythmic direction. In another Mozart example (from **4.6**), the goal points are the dissonances on the third beat, goals that the preceding turns and passing tones help to prepare, and from which the falling fourth intervals gracefully recede. The movement of preparation and resolution also brings the element of *rubato* into play, with the dissonant notes and their resolutions sometimes demanding a fraction more time than the metronome would allow them.

EXAMPLES

In the following three excerpts from Mozart, make reductions as suggested, identify the embellishing tones, and use the practice methods above to help you realize the full expressive value of the melodic dissonances.

4.5 Mozart: Piano Sonata in A, K. 331, I, Var. III, 1–4

Try using the Repeat and React method, repeating blocked chords underneath each melody note to find and appreciate the dissonant ones. Compare the expressive effects of accented vs. unaccented passing tones, and upper vs. lower neighbor tones.

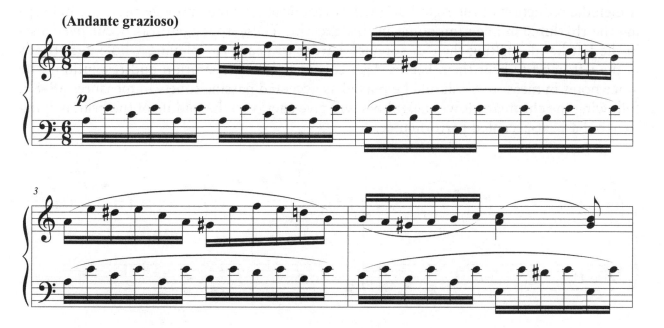

4.6 Mozart: Piano Sonata in F, K. 332, II, 1–4

If you make an outer voice reduction of this passage, you should find some of the patterns familiar from Chapter 2. Use Repeat and React again to hear the dissonant melodic notes, as well as Prepare and Resolve to achieve rhythmic motion and good inflection. Add arrows, dynamic markings, and other annotations to indicate the inflection.

4.7 Mozart: Piano Concerto in D Minor, K. 466, I, 77–91

A melodic reduction of the right hand will reveal how vital the appoggiaturas are in keeping the rhythmic momentum going in this excerpt. These appoggiaturas occur over rests in the left hand, making their dissonance harder to hear. Try playing whole-note triads in the left hand to hear them better. Also consider their preparation and resolution. The grace notes in measure 87 should be played as accented passing tones. In measures 88–89, following the chromatic lower neighbors will give energy to the middle of the beat, helping to avoid a beat-accented performance.

SUSPENSIONS

4.8 Types of Suspensions

The chart below shows the main types of suspensions—single suspensions in the first line, double suspensions in the second. They are named by the intervals formed between the bass and the suspension and its resolution. Because they are the only embellishing tones that are "figured" in this way, they form an important part of figured bass accompaniment.

a. Single Suspensions

b. Double Suspensions

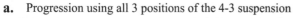

4.9 Progressions with Suspensions

Play the two progressions below first without the suspensions (move the resolution notes forward one quarter note) to hear the basic chords that are being embellished. Restore the suspensions, memorize the progressions, and transpose to other major keys (**b.** can also be played in minor, retaining the leading tone).

a. Progression using all 3 positions of the 4-3 suspension

b. Progression using the 4 main types of suspensions

4.10 Sequences with Suspensions

Here we embellish two of the sequences from Chapter 3, and parallel first inversion chords from Chapter 2. Memorize the patterns and transpose to other major keys. The first two can also be played in minor, retaining the leading tone at the cadence.

a. Descending seconds sequence with 9-8 suspensions

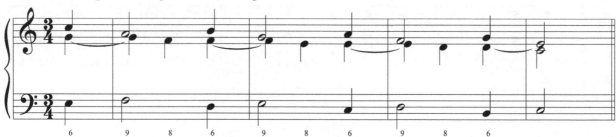

b. Parallel first inversion triads with 7-6 suspensions

c. Descending thirds sequence with 4-3 and 9-8 suspensions

4.11 Short Figured Basses with Suspensions

Play each short exercise first without the suspension and notice which voice has the resolution note of the suspension. For example, in the first exercise, if you start with F in the soprano as suggested, the third of the V chord (E) will be in the soprano. To add the suspension, simply delay that note by one beat. The suggested starting positions will give you practice in putting the suspensions in different voices, and allow you to connect the exercises to each other with good voice leading.

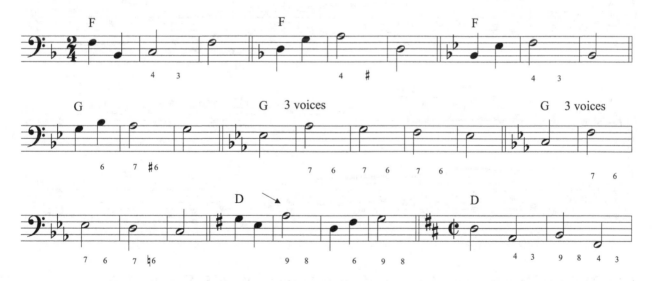

56 Embellishing Tones

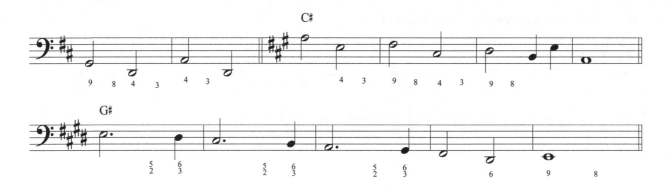

EXAMPLES WITH SUSPENSIONS

In the following examples, identify the suspensions with the appropriate figures (Roman numerals are unnecessary) and practice as suggested.

4.12 Haydn: Piano Sonata in A♭, Hob. XVI:46, II, 1–8

Use the Listen and Linger practice method to make sure that you hear the suspensions in this excerpt. Three of them have delayed, or ornamented, resolutions (shown with dotted slurs), which are also important to listen for.

4.13 Mozart: Variations on *Ah, vous dirai-je Maman*, K. 265, Var. VI, 1–8

Identify the suspensions and study the patterns of the passing and neighbor tones in the left hand. Reduce the whole passage to its basic chords, leaving out all the embellishing tones.

4.14 Bach: Little Prelude in F, BWV 927, 1–8

Reduce this passage to its essential harmonies and notice the change in harmonic rhythm at the approach to the cadence in measure 8. Identify the type of sequence Bach uses, and the suspensions that ornament it. The first three measures have a pedal point in the bass, also sometimes considered a non-chord tone.

4.15 Bach: French Suite No. 3 in B Minor, Sarabande, 1–8

Linger and Listen on the tied and syncopated notes to find and hear the suspensions better. Add dynamics, arrows, and articulation marks to indicate expressive inflections. Figure the bass and play a simple continuo accompaniment that leaves out the melody.

4.16 Figured Bass Reconstructions

Below, the three preceding examples are reduced to figured bass lines. Use them first to check your own figures, then to reconstruct the examples. Start by adding right-hand chords from the figures, which should give you something like the reductions you made directly from the examples. Then try to restore the details of the left hand, looking back to the originals to check anything that you are unsure of. Finally, restore the remaining right-hand detail, again looking back as needed. Make annotations above the figured bass to help you remember these details and play the complete passages while looking only at the annotated bass lines. You can also use these figured basses to play continuo accompaniments to another student's performance of the original.

Mozart Variation

Bach Prelude

Bach Sarabande

5 Second Inversion Triads

Second inversion triads are ornamental in nature, prolonging and embellishing the more stable chords that surround them. In this chapter, we study the ways in which these chords embellish some of the patterns we learned in Chapter 2, consider their inflection in performance, and begin to harmonize melodies using chords in the left hand.

5.1 Mozart: Piano Sonata in C, K. 330, II, 1–8

This excerpt contains four second inversion triads, indicated underneath the staff by their figured bass numbers, $^6_4$. One of them fills in a voice exchange (at the f in measure 2), while the other three embellish the principal cadences. All of them can be explained as double embellishing tones (as suggested by the analysis), but because they happen to form triads, we can also analyze them as chords, although giving them their own Roman numerals would obscure their ornamental nature. Their embellishing function is easily demonstrated by the fact that we can remove these chords (simply skip over them to their $^5_3$ resolutions) and observe that, while the expression is impoverished, the harmony still makes sense.

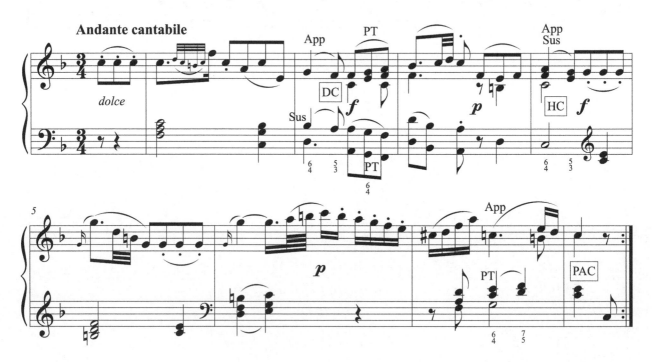

5.2 Types of Second Inversion Triads

The example below shows the four main types of $^6_4$ chords, which are named after the ornamental roles they play.

a. **Neighbor** $^6_4$: From a root position triad (usually I), two notes move up a step and back down (like neighbor tones), creating a IV$^6_4$ chord that prolongs I.
b. **Cadential** $^6_4$: This chord ornaments V at a half or authentic cadence. Although it is a tonic chord in second inversion, it has a dominant function because it prolongs V.
c.–e. **Passing** $^6_4$: This chord fills in a voice exchange, connecting a root position triad (usually I) to the same chord in first inversion (**c.**). It can also connect IV^6 to ii^6 (**d.**), or form part of a double voice exchange (**e.**).
f. **Pedal** $^6_4$: This is another kind of passing $^6_4$, connecting V to V^7, prolonging the dominant on a pedal point.

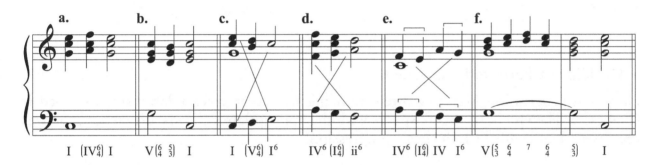

EXERCISES

5.3 Progressions

Memorize the following three progressions and transpose them to other keys, going counterclockwise around the circle of fifths (continue with F major, D minor, B♭ major, etc.). Aim for a smooth connection of chords and clean pedaling.

62 Second Inversion Triads

5.4 Adding $^6_4$ Chords to Progressions

Play each progression first as written, noticing the outer voice relationships studied in Chapter 2. Then fill in the blank spaces with the appropriate $^6_4$ chords, listening to the way they extend and embellish the basic progressions.

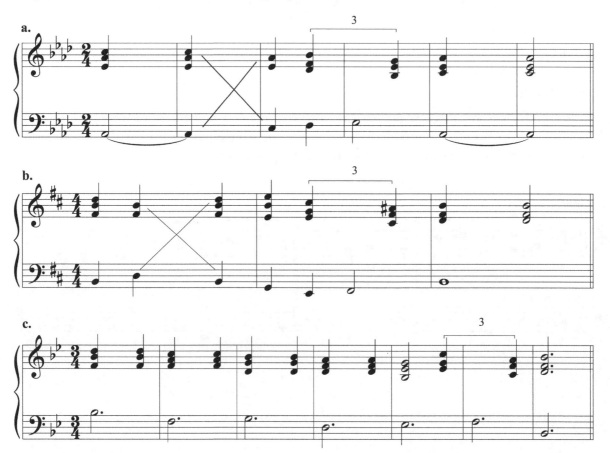

5.5 Figured Bass

Find the best positions for the right hand by first leaving out the $^6_4$ chords and looking for parallel first inversion triads, voice exchange, and falling thirds, then adding the $^6_4$ chords.

PERFORMANCE CONSIDERATIONS

5.6 The Influence of the Overtones

Second inversion triads often constitute a high point of tension within a phrase. This is due to the relative dissonance of its two intervals—the sixth and fourth—above the bass. The overtones of the bass pull these two intervals down to the fifth and third, making the fundamental inflection of second inversion triads to their resolutions one of *diminuendo*. This tension and resolution can be verified with the following experiment.

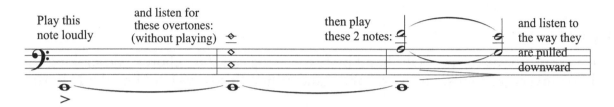

5.7 Inflection of ⁶₄ Chords

The inflection of second inversion triads is akin to that of the embellishing tones whose names they share.

- **Neighbor** ⁶₄ chords, like neighbor tones, stand out from their surroundings, producing a swell of sound toward and away from them (< >), as in the opening of Bach's Prelude in G, BWV 902.

- **Cadential** ⁶₄ chords function as double suspensions or appoggiaturas and should be inflected in the same way—prepared by the notes that precede them, and resolved with a *diminuendo*. Because of the appoggiatura's "reaching" quality, there is often an element of *rubato* involved as well (shown with wavy lines below). After the resolution, there is frequently a breath (comma) to articulate the phrasing. The Mozart phrase from **5.1** illustrates all these considerations.

- **Passing** $^6_4$ chords, like passing tones, have a flowing forward motion, even when they are nominally in an accented rhythmic position, as in the beginning of "January," from "The Seasons" by Tchaikovsky.

EXAMPLES

Play each of the four passages below and do the following:
- **Analyze** the types of $^6_4$ chords, important embellishing tones, outer voice patterns from Chapter 2 (parallel 6, voice exchange, and falling third), and cadences.
- **Inflect** the second inversion triads and embellishing tones as suggested in **5.7** and **4.3**. Add annotations (wavy lines, commas, arrows, dynamics, etc.) to illustrate your understanding.
- **Reduce** the passage to an outer voice reduction (see **2.3** for a reminder of how to do this). This can be either written down or played.

5.8 Mozart: Piano Sonata in D, K. 311, II, 1–8

66 Second Inversion Triads

5.9 Beethoven: Piano Sonata in F Minor, Op. 2, No. 1, II, 1–8

5.10 Beethoven: Piano Sonata in F Minor, Op. 2, No. 1, IV, 62–71

5.11 Mendelssohn: Song Without Words, Op. 85, No. 3, 1–5

5.12 Melodic Reconstructions

Below, the four passages above are reduced to their main melodic lines, with many of the embellishing tones and $^6_4$ chords represented as grace notes to better show their ornamental roles. Compare these reductions to the ones you made yourself, then reconstruct the bass lines with the aid of the annotations, looking back to the originals if there are places of which you are unsure. Next, restore the middle voices and remaining melodic detail, trying as much as possible to look only at the reduction. Finally, try playing the passages entirely from memory.

68 *Second Inversion Triads*

Beethoven Prestissimo

Mendelssohn

LEFT-HAND ACCOMPANIMENT

5.13 Melody and Accompaniment Style in Close Position

All the exercises we have done so far have been in keyboard style, with chords in the right hand, but it is of course very common in keyboard music for the chords to be in the left hand, accompanying a melody in the right hand. When the chords fit into the left hand without stretching or jumping, it is called close position. When the chords are more widely spaced and the left hand must jump to reach them, it is called spread position. Close position is considerably easier, so we will begin with that.

With inverted triads, voice leading with the left hand alone is very simple, as we know from the chord progression that all children learn (**a.**, below). The only real difficulty is when there are two consecutive root position triads (I and V, for example), which produce large leaps and parallel fifths (**b.**). The most common solutions are shown in **c.** and **d.**, with **e.** showing a frequent variant using the cadential $^6_4$.

In the four melodies that follow, the annotations will help you to find the missing chords. At this stage, our focus with melody harmonization is not so much to guess what the chords are as to conceptualize the harmony in a way that makes learning music a deliberate analytical act, rather than the haphazard result of repeated readings. Once you have found the chords, consider the inflection of the embellishing tones, using the practice methods from Chapter 4, as well as the inflection of the $^6_4$ chords discussed in this chapter.

5.14 Clementi

Note that only some of the chords are given, not the more obvious ones.

5.15 Mozart

The brackets indicate a sequence (see Chapter 3).

5.16 Mozart

Note that the key signature reflects the key of the piece, but not of this particular passage.

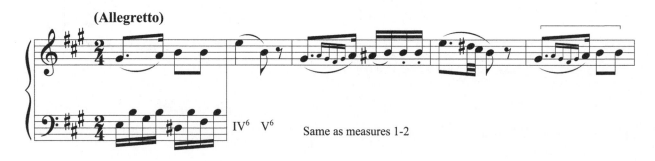

Second Inversion Triads 71

5.17 Mozart

Use an alberti bass accompaniment such as the one in **5.16**.

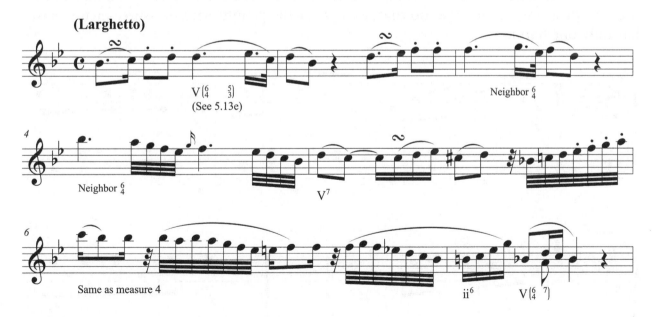

6 The Dominant Seventh Chord in Root Position

Adding a minor seventh to the major triad on the dominant creates a powerfully dissonant chord that cries out for resolution to the tonic. This tonality-defining chord is so important and pervasive that we will devote three chapters to it. In this chapter, we will study the voice leading principles of the root position dominant seventh chord and its resolution, while learning a new style of left-hand accompaniment—the spread position, or leaping left hand.

6.1 Schubert: *Valse Sentimentale*, D. 779, No. 18

Schubert wrote hundreds of these short dances in binary form—Waltzes, German Dances, Ländler, and Ecossaises. Many of them contain bold harmonic surprises, while others, like this one, use only the tonic and dominant chords, with perhaps an occasional subdominant. This one contains most of the elements we will study in this chapter, including the spread position left-hand accompaniment. Notice how Schubert leaves the leading tone out of the left hand whenever it is present in the right hand (compare, for example, measure 3 to measure 7). Observe too that, except for the penultimate measure, each measure has only one harmony.

DOI: 10.4324/9781003333289-7

6.2 Voice Leading Principles

The dominant seventh chord (V^7) is formed by adding a minor seventh above the bass to a root position dominant triad (**a.**). The addition of the minor seventh (scale degree $\hat{4}$) creates the interval of a tritone with the leading tone ($\hat{7}$), which when spelled as a fifth resolves inward to a third, and when spelled as a fourth resolves outward to a sixth (**b.**). In four-voice harmony, one can double the root of the V^7 chord, leaving out the fifth of the chord. This is called an incomplete V^7, which resolves to a complete tonic chord (**c.**). Alternatively, one can use all four notes of the V^7 chord (a complete V^7), which in strict four-part writing resolves to an incomplete tonic chord (**d.**). This is somewhat uncommon in keyboard music, so we will use primarily the incomplete V^7.

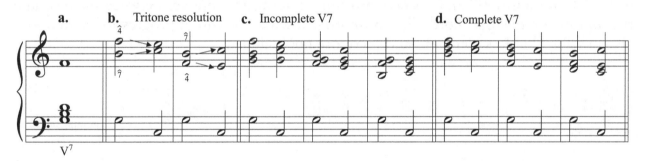

EXERCISES

6.3 Chord Shapes

The introduction of the seventh creates some chord shapes we have not yet studied. It's a good idea to make these automatic before proceeding any further. Play these three positions of the incomplete V^7 chord without looking at your hands, using the common notes between the chords (shown with lines below) to help guide you across the keyboard. Proceed upward by half steps (A♭ V^7, A V^7, etc.).

6.4 Resolutions

This example shows all six possible positions of the root position V⁷ chord and their resolutions in keyboard style. Memorize the voice leading and chord shapes and transpose them to several keys. With the incomplete V⁷ (**a.**), use the common tone on $\hat{5}$ as a tactile aid for moving across the keyboard without looking at your hands. The complete V⁷ (**b.**) will not be used in this chapter, but is included for reference. The two-note resolutions in the right hand are a result of the D and B ($\hat{2}$ and $\hat{7}$) converging on a unison C.

6.5 Progression with Incomplete V⁷

Play the following progression in all 24 keys, going counterclockwise around the circle of fifths. "Tenth position" and "octave position" refer to the interval between the bass and the soprano on the first chord. Fifth position (shown at the end of progression **a.** in **6.4**) is also possible, but less common, and therefore not included.

6.6 Converting Keyboard Style to Spread Position Accompaniment

If you play the left hand of the Schubert Waltz in **6.1** with two hands (bass in the left hand, chord in the right), you will see that spread position accompaniment is essentially the same as keyboard style four-voice harmony. In this style of accompaniment, some adjustments must be made to accommodate the melody, but the basic rules of voice leading are the same as those for keyboard style harmony. A good way to learn to play spread position accompaniments is therefore to play them first with two hands, in keyboard style, then with the left hand alone, using a waltz rhythm pattern. The examples below illustrate how to practice the figured bass exercises in **6.7**, and the melody harmonizations that follow, in this way.

a.

An 8 above the first bass note means the first chord is in octave position.

Play the progression with 2 hands...

...then with the left hand alone. Stop the rhythm on the downbeat of the last chord.

b.

A 10 above the first bass note means the first chord is in tenth position.

In 10th position, stop the rhythm on the second beat of the last bar.

c. If there is a leading tone in the melody, leave it out of the left hand, and play the fifth of the chord instead.

Note that Schubert avoids this position:

d. Sometimes a change of chord is required on the third beat of the measure.

6.7 Figured Bass

These figured basses provide exercise in the patterns we will use to accompany the Schubert melodies that follow. Practice them with two hands first, as shown in **6.6**, then with the left hand alone, using a waltz accompaniment. All the V^7 chords should be incomplete, as in **6.5** and **6.6**. The letters "LT" above a bass note means that there is, hypothetically, a leading tone in the melody, which must therefore be omitted from the left hand and replaced with the fifth of the chord (as in **6.6c.**). Once you can play these accompaniments easily with the left hand, compose or improvise a melody in the right hand.

76 *The Dominant Seventh Chord in Root Position*

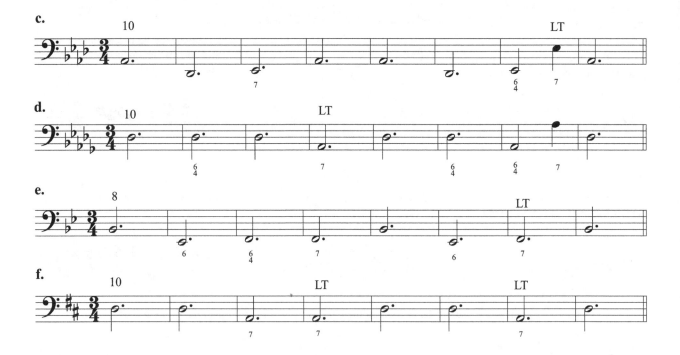

MELODY HARMONIZATIONS

The following dances by Schubert use only a limited number of chords—the tonic in root position and occasionally in second inversion, the V^7 in root position (always incomplete), and the IV chord in root position and second inversion. Roman numerals are given in places where the correct chord may not be obvious. The starting position for the first chord is also provided. Remember that a two-note slur over a descending second usually indicates that the first note is an embellishing tone. Play the melody first, determine the chords, then practice the accompaniment first with two hands, then with the left hand alone, as in **6.6** and **6.7**.

6.8 Schubert: Ländler in A♭

6.9 Schubert: German Dance in D

6.10 Schubert: Ländler in D♭

The B♭ in measure 3 (and in measure 7) adds a ninth to the V⁷ chord, a frequent occurrence in Schubert.

6.11 Schubert: Ländler in G

78 The Dominant Seventh Chord in Root Position

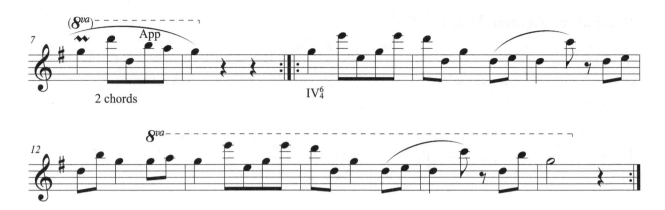

6.12 Schubert: German Dance in A♭

6.13 Schubert: Ecossaise in A♭

In Ecossaises, play the bass note on the first beat and the chord on the second.

6.14 Schubert: Ecossaise in D♭

Start in octave position

Change to 10th position

6.15 Schubert: Unfinished Ländler, D. 374, No. 6

6.16 Schubert: Unfinished Ländler, D. 370, No. 4

7 Inversions of the Dominant Seventh Chord

Whereas the root position dominant seventh chord is frequently used to mark the cadence at the end of a phrase with a descending fifth (or ascending fourth) in the bass, inversions of that chord generate stepwise bass lines that create cohesion and forward motion within the phrase. In this chapter, we will study all three inversions of the V^7 chord, using all three of the harmonic styles we have practiced so far—keyboard style, left-hand chords in close position, and spread position accompaniment.

7.1 Schubert: Impromptu in A♭, D. 935, No. 2

In this excerpt, Schubert uses all three inversions of the dominant seventh chord (identified in the example by their figured bass numbers) to create a smooth, melodic bass line and a sense of flowing forward motion. The root position V^7 is saved until the end, to bring the section to a close. The secondary dominant chord (see Chapter 8) just before this concluding cadence is all the more beautiful for being the only chromatic moment in this otherwise diatonic section. Play the outer voices—only the melody and the bass line—to hear the counterpoint they make together.

Because the voice leading of inverted dominant seventh chords uses entirely stepwise motion, these chords are often regarded as embellishing chords of the tonic harmonies they resolve to. We even use the language of embellishing tones to describe them—neighbor $^6_5$ and passing $^4_3$, for example. Furthermore, their inflection in performance is similar to that of their corresponding non-chord tones—neighbor chords, like neighbor tones, produce a "swell" in the sound (< >), while passing chords, like passing tones, lead forward by filling in a gap. Play the bass line below with the suggested inflections (which should be discreet and subtle), then play the complete original to hear how this inflection of the bass line guides the melody through each phrase, and all the way to the final cadence.

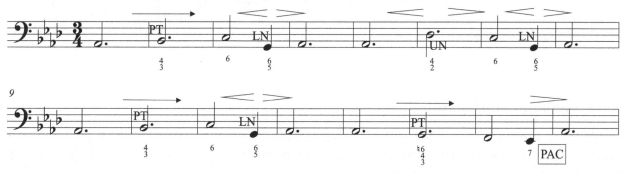

EXERCISES

7.2 Embellishing Functions of Inverted Dominant Seventh Chords

The example below summarizes the embellishing roles played by the three inversions of V^7. The right-hand positions given are the ones most commonly used, with either $\hat{4}$ (the seventh of the chord) or $\hat{7}$ (the leading tone) in the soprano. Memorize these progressions and transpose them to other major and minor keys.

- **First Inversion** ($^6_5$) functions as a neighbor chord to I. The bass makes a lower neighbor (LN) motion while two of the upper voices make upper neighbor motions (**a.**).
- **Second Inversion** ($^4_3$) can be either a neighbor chord to I with an upper neighbor (UN) in the bass (**b.**) or a passing chord on the way to I^6 (**c.**). Note the exceptional upward resolution of the seventh in this progression, justified to avoid doubling the third on I^6.
- **Third Inversion** ($^4_2$) can be either a neighbor chord to I^6 (**d.**) or arise from a passing tone from V to I^6 (**e.**).

82 *Inversions of the Dominant Seventh Chord*

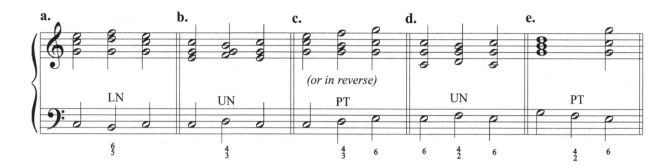

Dominant seventh inversions are frequently paired together, forming a four-chord unit with tonic bookends. Depending on the inversions used, the two dominant chords make either a double neighbor figure (**f.** and **g.**) or a neighbor plus cadence with V^7 (**h.** and **i.**). Memorize and transpose these patterns as well.

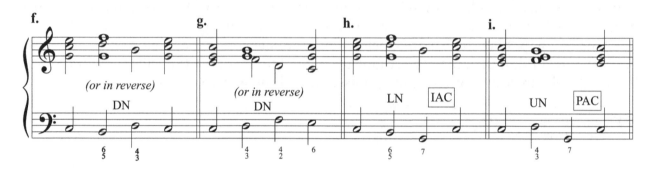

7.3 Resolutions in All Positions

While the right-hand positions given in **7.2** are the most common, all three positions are used. In the interest of completeness, these are given below. Note that in all three inversions, the individual voices always move in the same way: $\hat{7} \to \hat{1}$, $\hat{4} \to \hat{3}$, $\hat{2} \to \hat{1}$, and $\hat{5} \to \hat{5}$, with the exception of $\hat{4} \to \hat{5}$ when V^4_3 resolves to I^6 (**c.**). It is also useful to remember that in inversions of the V^7 chord, the bass note is always left out of the right hand. To review the root position V^7 resolutions, see example **6.4**.

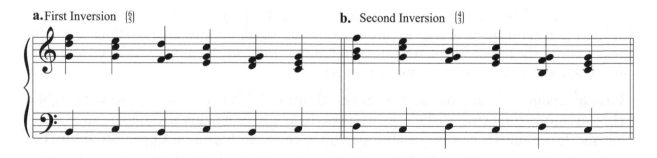

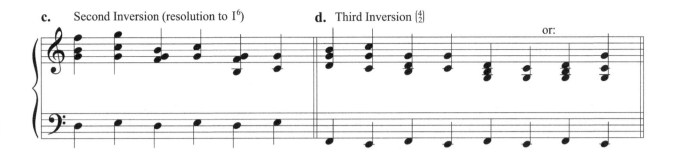

7.4 Figured Bass

Play these exercises in keyboard style. If you start each one in tenth position, the dominant seventh chords will be in their strongest positions, with the seventh of the chord in the soprano. Practice tip: To find the right-hand chord shapes more easily, first play all four notes of the dominant seventh chord in the right hand, then remove the bass note from the chord.

84 *Inversions of the Dominant Seventh Chord*

EXAMPLES

In each of the following examples, all by Beethoven and all in A♭ major, do the following:

- **Analyze** the dominant seventh chords, second inversion triads, any relevant outer voice patterns from Chapter 2, important embellishing tones, and cadences.
- **Inflect** the inverted dominant seventh chords as suggested in **7.1**, as well as the second inversion triads. Add dynamics and other annotations as needed.
- **Reduce** each passage to an outer voice reduction.

7.5 Beethoven: Piano Sonata in C Minor, Op. 10, No. 1, II, 1–8

7.6 Beethoven: Piano Sonata in E♭, Op. 27, No. 1, III, 4–7

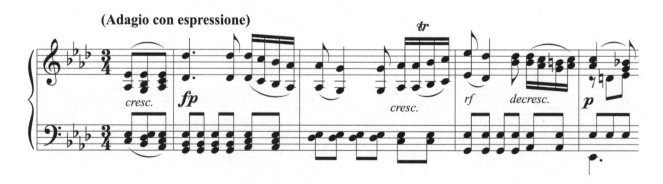

7.7 Beethoven: Piano Sonata in E♭, Op. 31, No. 3, II, 1–9

7.8 Melodic Reconstructions

Below, the three examples above are reduced to their main melodic notes. Add your own annotations (figured bass, outer voice relationships, etc.) to help you reconstruct the bass line. Next, add the inner voices, making particular note of the harmonic texture (how many notes in each hand). Add the remaining details and try to play the original passages while looking only at the reductions, then entirely from memory. Pay attention to the details that are hardest to memorize and try to find ways to describe them to make them easier to remember.

Op. 10, no. 1

Op. 27, no. 1

Op. 31, no. 3

ACCOMPANIMENT IN CLOSE POSITION

7.9 Mozart: Fantasy in D Minor, K. 397, 12–15

In close position accompaniment, we generally play three-note chords in the left hand, as we saw in Chapter 5. With four-note chords like the dominant seventh, that usually means we leave the melody note out of the left-hand chord, just as in keyboard style we left the bass note out of the right-hand chord. This is especially necessary when the leading tone or the seventh of the chord ($\hat{7}$ or $\hat{4}$) is in the melody, as these "tendency tones" should not be doubled. This phrase, from Mozart's Fantasy in D Minor, provides a good example of this issue, and also illustrates a classic double neighbor bass line.

7.10 Close Position Resolutions

The chart below shows all the possible left-hand accompaniments for the three melodic fragments that support a V^7–I resolution. Memorize these patterns so that you can use them in the two melody harmonizations that follow.

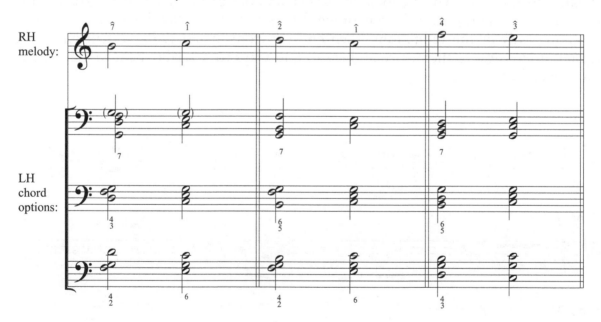

7.11 Mozart

Add a left-hand accompaniment in close position. Some of the V^7 inversions are specified; others can be inferred from the melody. You may find it helpful to write in the letter names of the bass notes and practice the bass line together with the melody. *Tacet* is Latin for "silent."

7.12 Haydn

In this example, the left-hand accompaniment is described in detail so that you can find the harmonies without having them explicitly written out.

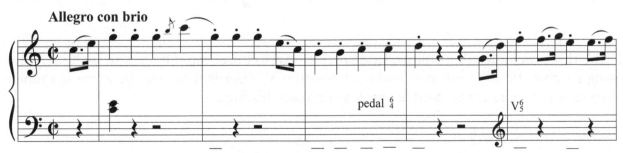

Add 2-3 note chords in the blank spaces

88 *Inversions of the Dominant Seventh Chord*

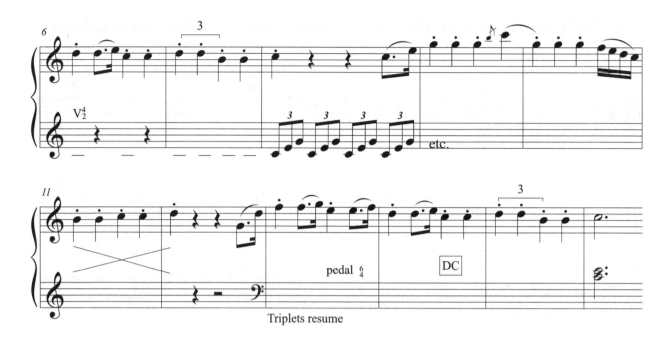

ACCOMPANIMENT IN SPREAD POSITION

7.13 Schubert: Ländler, D. 734, No. 12, 1–4

Spread position accompaniment, as we saw in Chapter 6, is like four-voice keyboard style harmony, only it is played entirely by the left hand. We have already seen how Schubert omits the leading tone from the V^7 chord when that note is in the melody (see **6.1**, for example). With inverted V^7 chords, we would obviously not put the leading tone in the bass if it were already in the melody, but Schubert doesn't mind if it is present in an inner voice. In this example, he uses the leading tone in the V^4_3 chord of measure 2, but avoids it in the V^7 that follows. (However, see **7.18** for Chopin's response to the same issue.)

In the three melodies that follow, add spread position accompaniments in waltz rhythm, using combinations of inverted and root position V^7 chords. Practice the accompaniment alone using two hands to double check your voice leading.

7.14 Schubert: Waltz in C♯ Minor

Note that the second half is in the relative major.

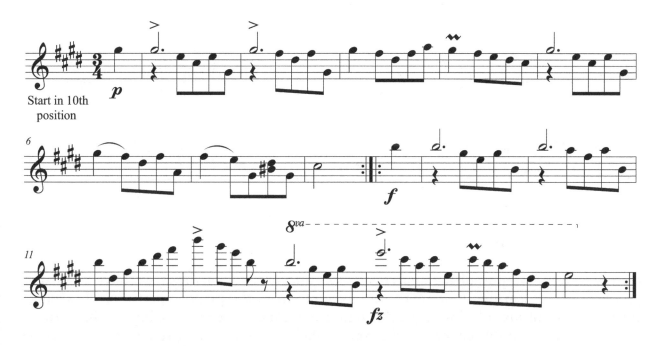

7.15 Schubert: Unfinished Ländler, D. 370, No. 5

7.16 Schubert: Unfinished Ländler, D. 355, No. 3

The chord in measure 5 may look as if it should be iv, but the grace note suggests that it is more likely a dominant seventh chord.

90 Inversions of the Dominant Seventh Chord

REPERTOIRE STUDY

In this section, we put all the analytical tools and practice methods we have studied to practical use in learning more extended excerpts from the piano repertoire. "Learning" them means not just playing them through a few times, but recognizing all the patterns we have studied, in this chapter and in the preceding ones; making reductions to uncover the essential harmonic framework; separating the different strands of the texture to hear them better; sharpening our ears to appreciate the dissonance of embellishing tones; and finally combining all of these to memorize the excerpt and play it with natural expression and informed understanding.

While the final product of this study is a polished, memorized performance, documenting your practice is also important. Writing out your reductions, penciling in performance nuances, noting your analysis in the score—all of these will help you to practice more deliberately and consciously. The suggestions given for each excerpt are just to get you started, and are not exhaustive.

7.17 Beethoven: Rondo in C, Op. 51, No. 1, 1–17

Suggested Practice Methods: Outer voice reduction, reduced bass line with melody as written.
Analysis: Look especially at the bass line patterns and outer voice relationships, analyze the cadences.
Inflection: Add more dynamic nuances.

7.18 Chopin: Waltz, Op. 69, No. 2, 1–16

Suggested Practice Methods: Melody as written with just the bass line, left-hand accompaniment played with two hands (both of these are also excellent memory tests).

Analysis: Bass line patterns, embellishing tones (use Repeat and React to find and hear them better). Describe passages that may be difficult to analyze (e.g., measures 6–8) in your own words.

Inflection: Consider *rubato* (relate it to the harmony and the embellishing tones).

92 Inversions of the Dominant Seventh Chord

8 Secondary Dominant Chords

In Chapters 6 and 7, we studied the primary dominant seventh chord, the one built on $\hat{5}$ and resolving to the tonic. The dominant seventh chord is also frequently used as a secondary chord that can be "applied" to any of the other major and minor triads in a key (V^7 of V, for example). These important chromatic chords add color, tension, and rhythmic direction to harmonic progressions. In this chapter, we also delve deeper into the practice of transposition.

8.1 Mozart: Piano Sonata in D, K. 311, III, 206–221

In this sixteen-measure period, the antecedent phrase (measures 206–213) is almost entirely diatonic (with only one alteration in measure 210), while the consequent phrase is enriched by four secondary dominant chords. Notice the way these chords fill in the bass line with stepwise motion, and how their rhythmic position on the "weak" beats, or unaccented parts of beats, drive the motion forward to the strong beats.

94 Secondary Dominant Chords

EXERCISES

8.2 Progressions

The voice leading of secondary dominant seventh chords is the same as for the primary dominant seventh chord. As in V^7, the third of the chord (the secondary leading tone) and the seventh form a tritone, which resolves in contrary motion, outward when spelled as a fourth, inward when spelled as a fifth (**a.**). Secondary dominant chords may be complete or incomplete in root position, depending on how they are approached (**a.**). All of the inversions are also available (**b.**).

Note that all of the alterations in **a.** and **b.** are raising accidentals (sharps in the key of C), which create an increase in tension. In the major mode, only V/IV has a lowering accidental (for the seventh of the chord), which creates a decrease in tension (**c.**). Similarly, in the minor mode, the move toward the relative major (V/III) which doesn't require any accidentals at all, has a calming effect (**d.**). Follow the ebb and flow of these movements of tension and release as you play. Memorize these progressions before attempting to transpose them.

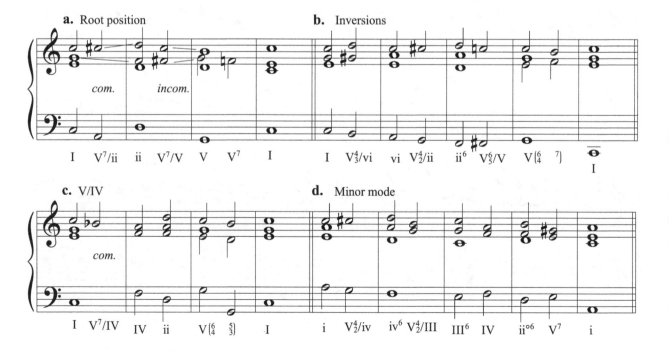

8.3 Transposing the Progressions

When we transpose, we cannot simply read the notes from the page as we normally do. Instead, we are forced to use our ears and our analytical skills, thinking more about the relationships of the notes to each other than about their individual names. This is precisely what makes transposition such a valuable skill for hearing, understanding, and assimilating the music we play.

Below, the four progressions in **8.2** are converted to templates that facilitate an analytical method of transposition. The rhythm of the progression is given on a single line, and the bass line is written in scale degrees below this line, with the Roman numerals above it. A four-step method for practicing is shown just below the templates.

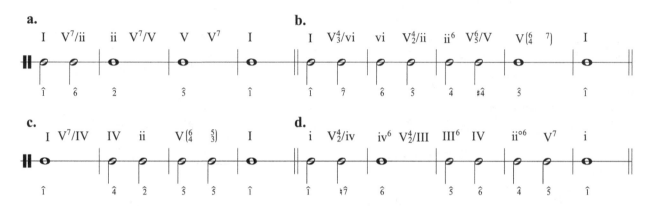

How to practice: Example transposing progression **a.** to D major.

1. Find the bass line using scale degrees or intervals.

2. Convert the Roman numerals to letter names in the new key, while playing only the bass.

3. Find the soprano, again by scale degrees or intervals.

4. Add the middle voices and think the voice-leading.

EXAMPLES

As you play the following two examples by Beethoven, notice the rhythmic placement of both the primary and the secondary dominant chords, which almost always fall on the second beat, and feel how this drives the rhythmic motion forward across the bar line.

8.4 Beethoven: Piano Concerto No. 4, Op. 58, II, 6–13

Play the excerpt, then use the template below it to transpose it to D minor and F minor. Practice as described in 8.3.

8.5 Beethoven: Piano Sonata in C Minor, Op. 13, II, 1–8

Play this excerpt in block chords, keeping the sixteenth notes in the right hand throughout, then transpose it to G and B♭ using the template below the excerpt.

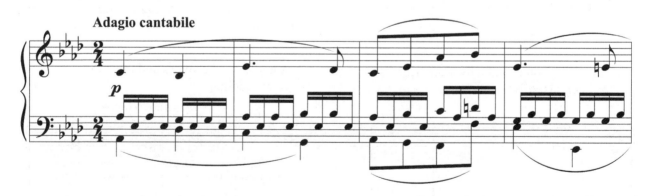

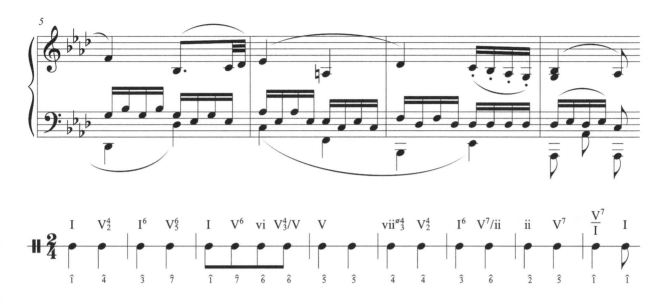

SEQUENCES

8.6 New Variations

The three kinds of sequences we studied in Chapter 3 can be enhanced by the addition of secondary dominants. The two-chord sequential unit, or cadence, can be used in different inversions and right-hand positions, making possible a great many variations. The four examples below are merely a small sample of the possibilities. Play them and study their patterns before transposing them as suggested in **8.7**.

a. **Descending Seconds:** This sequence is most often found in minor. If you stop on the fourth step of the sequence, the bass will have returned to V, making a good cadence point.

b. **Ascending Seconds in Major:** This sequence may be continued for an entire octave, skipping only the V/vii (secondary dominant chords cannot be applied to diminished triads), before returning to the opening pair of chords. Note the chromatic scale in the soprano, with the exception of the repeated note on $\hat{3}$.

98 Secondary Dominant Chords

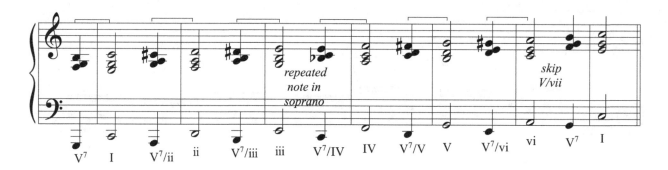

c. **Ascending Seconds in Minor:** In minor, it is difficult to continue for a full octave because of the ambiguity of the sixth and seventh scale degrees. We skip V/ii, again to avoid the diminished triad.

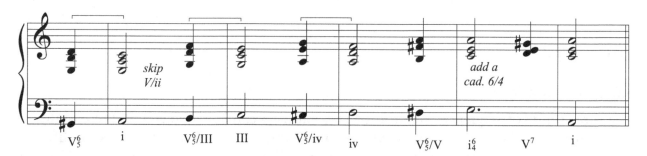

d. **Descending Thirds:** This is a common sequence in major. It normally stops after four steps, when it reaches ii, because a fifth step would take us to a diminished triad.

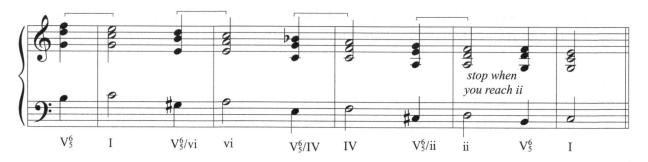

8.7 Transposing the Sequences

The sequences above can be transposed easily by thinking of them as ascending or descending staircases, upon each step of which we apply the same two-chord unit, or cadence. The outlines below should make it easier to transpose these sequences in this way. A three-step method for practicing is shown just after the outlines.

a. **Descending Seconds:**

$$\begin{array}{l}\underline{\quad}\ i \\ \quad \underline{\quad}\ \flat VII \\ \qquad \underline{\quad}\ VI \\ \qquad\quad \underline{\quad}\ V\text{-{}-{}-}V^7\text{-{}-{}-}i \end{array}$$

Secondary Dominant Chords 99

b. **Ascending Seconds in Major:**

```
                                              ___ I
                                        ___ vi
                                   ___ V
                             ___ IV
                       ___ iii
                 ___ ii
           ___ I
```

c. **Ascending Seconds in Minor:**

```
                       ___ V (cad. 6/4 --- V) --- i
                 ___ iv
           ___ III
     ___ i
```

d. **Descending Thirds:**

```
     ___ I
           ___ vi
                 ___ IV
                       ___ ii
                             ___ I
```

How to practice: Example transposing sequence a. (descending seconds) to G minor.

1. Play only the resolution chords
   (the chords in the outlines).

   i   ♮VII   VI   V

2. Add the bass notes of the secondary
   dominant chords (in this case, a fifth
   above each resolution note).

3. Add the secondary dominant chords in the right hand, and cadence.

8.8 Chopin: Mazurka, Op. 6, No. 4, 9–12

Reduce this example to block chords and compare it to the sequence in **8.6a**. How is it similar, and how different? Transpose the reduction to D minor and F minor, then restore the detail.

Highlight and Hear: In passages like this, it is often the inner voices that are most difficult to hear, and therefore to transpose or memorize. One way to help the ear hear these lines better is to highlight them, either by singing them as you play, or by playing them slightly louder than the other voices in the texture. Try this first with the alto voice (the right thumb), then with the tenor (the left thumb).

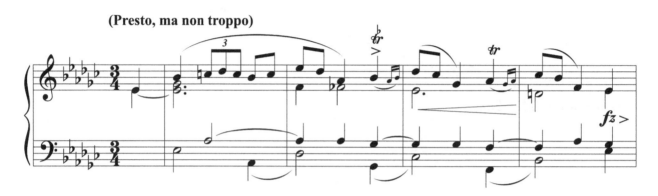

8.9 Schumann: Romanze, Op. 28, No. 1, 1–8

Reduce this example to block chords, leaving out the note following each octave in the left hand. Compare it to the sequence in **8.6c**. Try using the Highlight and Hear method with the line second from the top in the right hand. How are the rhythmic positions of the secondary dominant chords and the accent markings Schumann uses related to the harmony? Transpose the reduction to A minor and C minor, then restore the detail.

8.10 Schubert: German Dance, D. 420, No. 12, 1–8

Reduce this example to block chords and compare it to the sequence in **8.6d**. How are the *fp* markings related to the harmony? Transpose the reduction to G and B♭, then restore the detail.

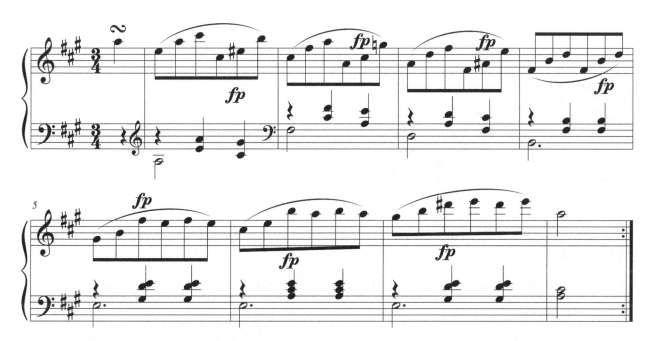

FILL-IN-THE-BLANK EXERCISES

Understanding how their patterns work allows us to play sequences such as the ones in the following examples even when most of the notes are missing. This is a great advantage in both sight-reading and memorizing.

8.11 Beethoven

Identify the type of sequence, then add the missing left-hand chords and memorize the excerpt. Why does Beethoven use A♮s in measures 5 and 7?

8.12 Schubert

Identify the type of sequence, then continue the left-hand pattern. Memorize.

8.13 Beethoven

Continue the pattern as described and memorize the passage. Why does Beethoven skip V/iii?

8.14 Haydn

This example shows the complete development section of a Haydn Sonata. The starting positions for each step of the sequences are given. All the sequences, except the last one, contain secondary dominant chords, and will therefore require the addition of accidentals.

104 *Secondary Dominant Chords*

REPERTOIRE STUDY

As in Chapter 7, the object in this section is to learn these two pieces from start to finish, using all the techniques and understanding you have acquired so far. As before, the suggestions below are just a beginning.

8.15 Johann Christoph Friedrich Bach: Solfeggio in D from *Musical Leisure Hours*

The composer clearly modeled this little piece on his father's Prelude in C major from Book 1 of the *Well-Tempered Clavier* (see **10.1**).

Suggested Practice Method: Blocked chords.
Analysis: Analyze the secondary dominants and sequence types; notice any slight changes of pattern (e.g., in measures 7–9).
Inflection: Add dynamic markings.
Transpose to C major.

8.16 Schumann: Arabesque, Op. 18, 1–40

Suggested Practice Methods: Melody and bass alone, chord reduction (blocked five-note chords), Highlight and Hear for inner voices (right thumbs, then left thumbs).

Analysis: Analyze secondary dominant chords, voice exchanges, and suspensions. The last two lines should be analyzed in G major.

Inflection: Rhythmic motion of dominant chords across the bar lines (notice slurs and tied notes).

Secondary Dominant Chords

9 Diatonic Modulation

Most music theory books describe modulation—the move from one key to another—as a technical process, which of course it is, but it is also an expressive event that performers must respond to in their playing. In this chapter, we will consider both the technical and the musical aspects of diatonic modulation—that is, modulation to closely related keys employing diatonic chords—using cadence "feel" as a guide to expression and understanding.

9.1 Beethoven: Piano Sonata in E♭, Op. 7, III, 1–24

Like many scherzos and minuets, this movement modulates to the dominant in its first section. Establishing a new tonic a fifth higher always entails a heightening of harmonic tension, and here this increase of tension takes an especially dramatic form. The drama is played out in the cadences Beethoven uses: the first phrase ends with a half cadence, conventionally enough (measure 8); the opening phrase then starts again until a deceptive cadence brings the music to a halt (measure 12); this is followed by a short, tentative cadence that could be heard as either an imperfect authentic cadence in B♭, or as another half cadence in E♭ (measure 14); this cadence is then hammered out four times in a higher register, insisting on its belonging to B♭ (measures 15–19), which key is finally fully confirmed by the perfect authentic cadence at the end of the excerpt. In this way, the ambiguity of the cadence in measure 14, and its subsequent resolution, becomes the musical meaning of this passage, a meaning which the performer must try to express.

GENERAL PRINCIPLES

9.2 Cadence Feel

In music theory, we tend to analyze cadences in an intellectual way, looking for certain visible signs in the score. But as practicing musicians, we can also feel them instinctively when we play. We sense *where* they are by feeling the natural breathing places in the music, and we sense what *kind* they are by feeling their relative degrees of finality. Deceptive cadences and half cadences feel unfinished or open-ended (**a.** and **b.**, below); perfect authentic and plagal cadences feel more conclusive (**d.** and **e.**), and imperfect authentic cadences feel somewhere in between the two (**c.**). This cadence feeling can therefore tell us, usually quite reliably, what key we are in. If a cadence feels conclusive, its final chord is most likely the tonic; if it feels inconclusive, it probably ends on either the dominant or the submediant. The progression below combines the five cadence types and uses arrows to show their relative degrees of finality. Upward-pointing arrows indicate a suspended, inconclusive feeling; the forward-pointing arrow suggests continuation is needed; and downward-pointing arrows show resolution and repose. Practice the progression in various keys, trying to capture these different cadence feelings in your playing.

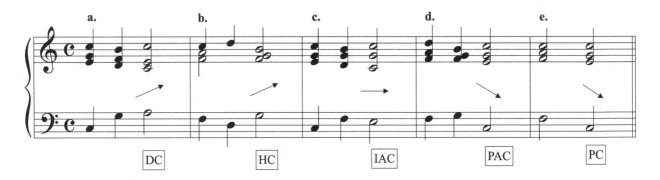

9.3 Pivot Chords

In the process of modulating to a new key, there is usually at least one chord that belongs to both the old key and to the new one. These pivot chords, as they are called, represent an interesting moment in musical perception. We usually don't realize that we are on a pivot chord while we are actually hearing it, but only afterwards, in retrospect, when the change of key is confirmed. The harmonic transformation is happening just beneath the surface of our consciousness. Nevertheless, there is often some kind of ripple effect on the surface of the music that portends the modulation that is just beginning to happen, often taking the form of an intensification, or change, in the rhythm or texture.

All of this is perfectly illustrated in the Mozart example below, from the second movement of the Piano Sonata in C, K. 330. A somber four-measure phrase establishes F minor with simple tonic and dominant harmonies. We hear the D♭-major triad in measure 26 as VI in F minor (it shares two common notes with the F-minor triad), but in fact, this is the pivot chord that is going to bring about a modulation to the relative major, in which key it becomes IV, as shown in the analysis. Notice the change of texture in this measure—the right-hand melody is reduced from double to single notes while the left-hand rhythm changes to repeated eighth-note chords. The grace notes in the right hand add to the intensification of the pivot chord, which leads to the climax in measure 27, where the rhythm comes to a stop on an E♭ dominant seventh chord. This is the point when we fully realize that a modulation is occurring, though it still takes an authentic cadence in the new key to confirm this. As with the Beethoven example, the drama of this passage is played out in its modulation and cadences.

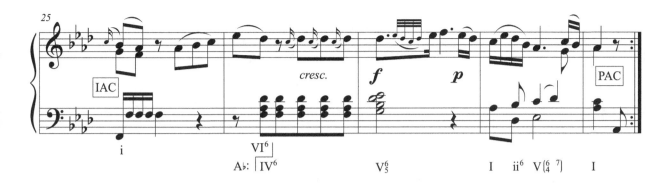

MODULATION TO THE DOMINANT

In major keys, the most common modulation is to the dominant. As already mentioned, moving the key up a fifth represents an increase of harmonic tension, which is often accompanied by changes in the rhythm or texture. The modulation back to the tonic (down a fifth), on the other hand, is much more relaxed, and the change of key is sometimes hardly perceptible. In the excerpts that follow, we will find the cadences and pivot chords, look for changes in texture and rhythm, and consider implications for performance. Since harmonic structure is most clearly revealed by the bass line, we will reduce most of these examples to just the melody and the bass.

9.4 Haydn: Piano Sonata (Divertimento) in G, Hob. XVI:8, II, 1–16

Play this minuet through, feeling the divisions (breathing points) in the phrasing as you play. Label the cadences and add arrows to show their inflection (as in **9.2**). Identify not only the obvious cadences at the double bars, but the internal ones as well. How do you show this musical "punctuation" in your playing? Identify the pivot chords and analyze the modulations (as in **9.3**). What changes accompany the modulation to the dominant, and how do you "activate" this modulation in performance?

9.5 Mozart: Piano Sonata in D, K. 284, III, 1–17

Play this passage, then analyze the cadences, modulations, pivot chords, and secondary dominants. Consider the inflection of the cadences (add arrows) and their appropriate articulation (add commas at breathing places). To feel how the bass line guides the phrase, reduce it to its main notes and play it together with the right-hand melody. This will also reveal the faster-moving harmonic rhythm at the cadences.

9.6 Schumann: *Erinnerung (In Memoriam)*, Album for the Young, Op. 68, No. 28, 1–10

In this example, the cadences are not quite as easy to see as in the previous two excerpts. Playing an outer-voice outline will help because the cadences occur on the longer bass notes. Label them as before (you should find five of them) and notice the way Schumann saves the most conclusive cadence for the end. Analyze the modulation as well as the secondary dominant chords. Also identify the embellishing tones and consider their inflection. The performance instructions mean "not fast and played in a very singing manner."

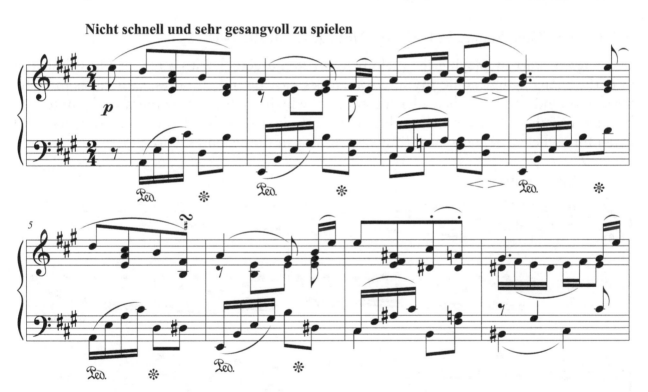

114 *Diatonic Modulation*

MODULATION TO THE RELATIVE MAJOR

In minor keys, the most common modulation is to the relative major. Because these two keys share the same key signature, accidentals are not required to bring about the modulation (though they may of course be present for other reasons). Consequently, this is a much less dramatic modulation than the one to the dominant. Instead, there is often a brightening of the mood as we pass into major, and a corresponding darkening when we return to minor.

9.7 Haydn: Piano Sonata in E Minor, Hob. XVI:34, III, 1–18

Once again, start by playing the melody as written together with a reduced bass line and note the changing harmonic rhythm, sometimes moving in half notes, sometimes in quarter notes. Find and label the cadences, some of which are hidden by the way the notes are beamed together. Analyze the modulations and pivot chords, identify the sequence, and listen for some particularly beautiful suspensions in the second section.

9.8 Schubert: German Dance, D. 783, No. 15

This short but highly expressive dance modulates to the relative major in each of its two halves (and back to the minor tonic at the repeats). What is the expressive climate of these two modulations, and what musical details accompany them (pivot chords, dynamics, etc.)? Also consider Schubert's almost obsessive use of the upper neighbor figure in the first half, and the rather unusual suspensions in the second half.

116 Diatonic Modulation

MODULATION TO THE RELATIVE MINOR

Of the remaining diatonic modulations, perhaps the most common one is from a major key to its relative minor. Normally, this modulation is not the only key change within a movement, but one among others, as in example 9.9.

9.9 Bach: French Suite No. 5 in G, Gavotte

The key scheme in this movement, which is given here in its entirety, is common in Bach's dance movements in binary form—from a major tonic, the music modulates to the dominant at the end of the first section, returns to the tonic at the beginning of the second section, then modulates to the relative minor, and back to the tonic to finish. After playing the movement through, identify the cadences and analyze the pivot chords. Also identify the two sequences and draw brackets over their units. Finally, play a continuo accompaniment to this movement and consider the harmonic rhythm: where do the chords last the longest, and where do they change more quickly?

All this information is tremendously helpful in devising an overall dynamic scheme for the movement, one of the principal interpretive decisions for a pianist performing Bach's music. Add dynamic markings to illustrate your decisions.

MELODY HARMONIZATIONS

Cadence feel can also help us to find the implied modulations in a given melody. In the following examples, play the melody by itself first, listening for the cadences and any key changes they may suggest. Once you have found the cadences and modulations, you can more easily fill in the remaining chords. Another useful practice method is to play the melody with only the bass line, not the entire chord. This helps to hear the linear character of the bass better. These melodies modulate only to the three key areas discussed above.

9.10 Czerny

Use an alberti bass accompaniment in eighth notes. In addition to a modulation, this example also contains secondary dominant chords of ii and IV.

9.11 Diabelli

This melody also uses an alberti bass accompaniment, and contains secondary dominants of V and iv in addition to the modulation.

9.12 Haydn

Add a simple bass line, similar to the one in **9.4**, using eighth notes and occasional quarter notes, especially at the cadences. Some of the outer voice patterns from Chapter 2 can be helpful here, as suggested at the beginning.

9.13 Beethoven

Use an accompaniment pattern like the one in **7.17**. Remember that the harmonic rhythm often speeds up just before the cadences.

9.14 Schubert

Use a waltz accompaniment in spread position for these last two melodies. The dynamic markings in this one can be of help in finding the harmonies.

9.15 Schubert

In addition to a modulation, this example also features an expressive change of mode in the second half (from minor to the parallel major).

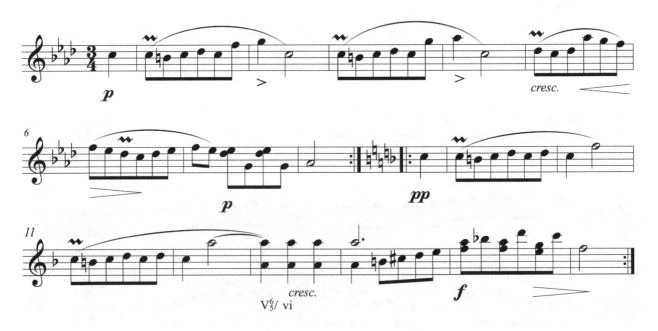

10 The Supertonic Seventh Chord

The supertonic seventh chord (ii^7), perhaps the most common seventh chord after the dominant, adds expressive warmth and harmonic dissonance to the pre-dominant triad on ii. In this chapter, we will relate the treatment of this dissonance to the preparation and resolution of suspensions, as discussed in Chapter 4. We will also practice chorale style harmony, revisit three practice methods that help us to hear dissonances better, and introduce a new technique for making exceptional harmonic events more vivid to our ears. Finally, we will further extend our practice of transposition to the interval of a descending third.

10.1 Bach: Prelude in C, *Well-Tempered Clavier*, Book 1, 1–19

This famous prelude relies heavily on the ii^7 chord, which lends harmonic tension and color at key points in its structure. The opening progression, using ii^7 in third inversion, is very common (measures 1–4). Following a sequence of descending seconds, another ii^7 chord, this time in root position, helps to define the new key of G at the cadence (measures 9–11). After another sequence of descending seconds takes us back to C major, the ii^7 chord again helps to confirm the modulation (measures 17–19). Play the passage through, noticing the way harmonic tension increases going into these ii^7 chords, and decreases as they resolve to V and on to I, thereby creating a natural dynamic scheme for the piece.

122 *The Supertonic Seventh Chord*

GENERAL PRINCIPLES

10.2 The Treatment of Dissonance

The seventh of the ii⁷ chord (and of all seventh chords, for that matter) is considered dissonant, and is normally treated in the same manner as a suspension—that is, the dissonant note is prepared by the same note in the preceding chord, and resolved down by step. The main difference is that with ii⁷, the dissonance and its resolution have two different chords (**a.**, below), whereas the suspension resolves within the same chord (**b.**).

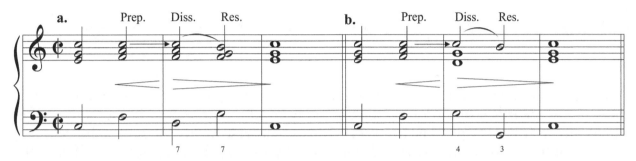

In the reduction of the Bach prelude shown below, the preparations of all the sevenths are shown with arrows, and the resolutions with slurs. As can be seen, these preparations and resolutions often overlap, and all of the voices except the middle one participate in this contrapuntal dovetailing of tension and release. To experience the horizontal ebb and flow of these lines, play the prelude with its sixteenth-note figuration while singing each of these voices. In a class setting, all the lines can be sung together as a choir. Listening to these individual lines in this way helps the pianist to inflect the harmony in a more subtle and nuanced manner than conventional dynamic markings can convey.

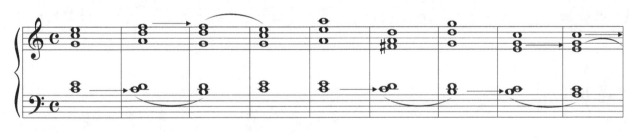

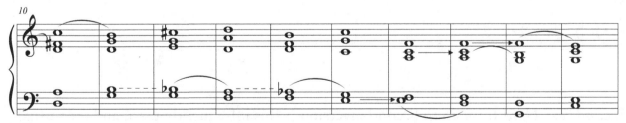

10.3 Resolutions and Voice Leading

The ii⁷ chord is used in both major and minor modes, in all three inversions, and in all three positions.

124 The Supertonic Seventh Chord

Root Position: Like the dominant seventh chord, the root position ii⁷ chord can be either complete (**a.**, below) or incomplete (**b.**). Because of the requirements of preparation and resolution, a complete ii⁷ will resolve to an incomplete V⁷, and vice versa.

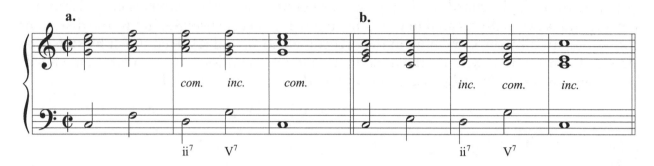

First Inversion: First inversion (ii$^6_5$) is by far the most frequently encountered type of ii⁷ chord. Its standard resolution is to the dominant triad (**c.**), to which the seventh is often added afterwards as a passing tone (**d.**). It can also resolve to V$^4_2$ simply by retaining the bass note (**e.**), or be transformed into V$^6_5$/V by raising the bass note a half step (**f.**). Occasionally, ii$^6_5$ resolves to the tonic rather than to the dominant, in a variation of the plagal cadence (**g.**). Finally, it is sometimes ornamented with an expressive 7–6 suspension (**h.**).

Second and Third Inversions: Second inversion (ii$^4_3$) is infrequently used, and then usually in the minor mode (**i.**). Note that the quality of the ii⁷ chord becomes half-diminished in minor. Third inversion (ii$^4_2$) resolves to V$^6_5$, as we saw in the Bach prelude (**j.**). Occasionally, it is used on a tonic pedal, usually in minor, in a variation of the neighboring $^6_4$ chord (**k.**).

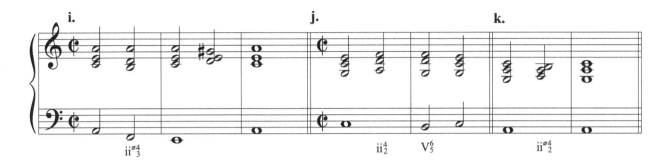

EXERCISES

10.4 Progressions

Practice these three progressions in all 24 keys, continuing counterclockwise around the circle of fifths. Progressions **a.** and **b.** alternate all three right-hand positions, while progression **c.** uses only two positions. Use your understanding of voice leading principles—common tones, preparation and resolution of the seventh, etc.—to help you transpose them, and be sure to inflect the movement of harmonic tension and release in your playing.

Progression **d.** uses some of the "other" resolutions of the ii⁷ chord (i.e., resolutions to chords other than V or V⁷). Transpose to other major keys.

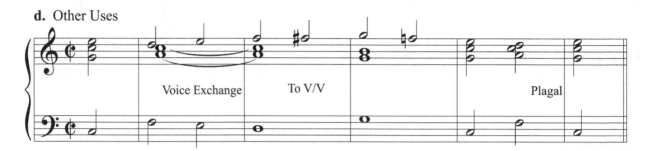

10.5 Chorale Style

Several of the examples in this chapter use a harmonic texture called chorale style, in which the voices are arranged in open position, in other words, with greater distance between them than in keyboard style, or close position. To convert keyboard style to chorale style, it is often possible simply to move the alto voice an octave lower into the left hand, as shown below.

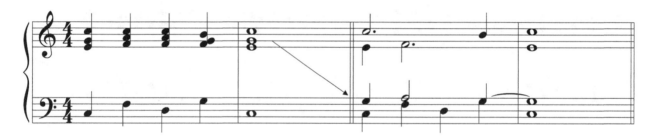

Playing in chorale style is more difficult than playing in keyboard style, but it is also more beautiful. The open spacing creates a richer sound, and having only two voices in each hand, rather than three in one hand, allows the player to connect the notes better and achieve a more contrapuntal independence of the parts.

Try converting some of the other progressions in **10.4** to chorale style, using the following practice routine.

1. Play the progression as written in keyboard style while singing the alto voice.
2. Move the alto an octave lower and play this voice (now the tenor) together with the bass, left hand alone. If the interval is too big to reach, move one or more bass notes an octave higher.
3. Play the right hand alone without the alto (middle) voice.
4. Play all four parts with both hands.
5. For greater rhythmic independence of the voices, hold the common tones rather than repeating them, as in the example above.

10.6 Figured Bass

These short figured basses can be played in both keyboard style and chorale style. As a preliminary step, play the chords in the left hand first, simply building the intervals upward from the bass. (This is just to find the chords; obviously, the voice leading is not good.) The first exercise, for example, would be played like this:

Next, work out the voice leading in keyboard style. Suggested starting positions are given. Lastly, convert keyboard style to chorale style using the technique described in **10.5**.

EXAMPLES

In the following examples, we introduce a new practice method, Replace and Restore, and revisit three practice methods first introduced in paragraphs **4.4** and **8.8**: Linger and Listen, Repeat and React, and Highlight and Hear. These methods help us to hear better the expressive and exceptional elements in the music, so that we may respond to them in our playing. We will also transpose these examples a third lower by replacing the bass clef with the treble clef.

10.7 Bach: Chaconne in D Minor for solo violin, transcribed for piano left hand by Brahms, 1–9

Find the ii⁷ chords, then indicate the preparation of the sevenths with arrows, and their resolutions with slurs. Transpose the excerpt to B minor by imagining the bottom staff in the treble clef, two octaves lower (with the new key signature, of course).

10.8 François Couperin: *Les Coucous bénévoles, Pièces de Clavecin, Ordre XIII*

Reduce this piece to block chords in chorale style to better feel the voice leading from chord to chord, then play as written. Analyze the harmony, then transpose it to G minor by imagining the lower staff in the treble clef (the D♯s will become B♮s in the new key). You can also replace the treble clef in the right hand with the soprano clef, if you have some familiarity with that clef. In any case, practicing the left hand first by itself, then both hands in block chords should make it easier.

Replace and Restore: Sometimes it is difficult to appreciate the exceptional nature and expressive quality of certain harmonic events because our ears have become habituated to their sounds. In such cases, it is instructive to try replacing the exceptional harmonies with more conventional ones. When we then restore the original chords, they once again sound fresh to our ears. In the Couperin, the colorful progression V^6/iv to ii$^6_5$ in measures 5–6 (and again in 13–14) can be replaced with the more ordinary progression i^6 to iv by changing D♯ to D♮ in measure 5 and C♯ to B in measure 6 (in the original key). Perhaps you also noticed some unusual voice leading in measures 3–4. What would the more conventional voice leading be? Try playing the piece with these alterations, then return to the original.

10.9 Mozart: Piano Concerto in C, K. 503, III, 171–178

First, play the piano part in block chords, feeling the common tones from chord to chord, and noticing the voice exchange between the left hand and right thumb notes in measures 174–176. Next, play the orchestral line together with the piano bass line, paying attention to the lovely embellishing tones in the melody. You can also sing the melody while playing the accompaniment.

Replace and Restore: Replace the B♮ in measure 176 with a B♭ to better appreciate the cross relation (the successive occurrence of a note and its chromatic alteration in different voices) this B♮ creates with the B♭ in measure 175. Also try singing the second voice from the top of the blocked piano chords to better follow the preparation and resolution of the seventh. What is irregular about the resolution of the cadential $^6_4$ in measure 177? Transpose the excerpt to D major, reading the lower staff in treble clef.

10.10 Schubert: Impromptu in E♭, D. 899, No. 2, 83–90

The two ii⁷ chords in this example resolve somewhat unusually back to the tonic rather than to the dominant. To better appreciate this exceptional usage, try replacing the ii$^4_2$ chord with a neighbor $^6_4$, and harmonize measure 89 with a V⁷ chord instead of ii$^4_3$. Transpose to G minor.

10.11 Chopin: Ballade in G Minor, Op. 23, 9–16

In this famous passage, the ii⁷ chord is used rather exceptionally as the end chord of a cadence (you could call it a plagal half cadence). Try replacing it with a iv chord to better appreciate its special color. How would you recompose the last four measures to be more conventional?

10.12 Schumann: Album for the Young, Op. 68, No. 30, 1–4

As in the Chopin above, this excerpt also uses the ii^7 chord at the cadence. Try the following practice methods.

Highlight and Hear: Sing the second voice from the top (the sustained F) while playing the excerpt.
Linger and Listen: Pause on the third beats of the first two full measures and listen to hear if the sustained F in the right hand (the seventh of the chord) is still sounding.
Repeat and React: Try repeating all the longer notes together with the shorter ones to hear all the dissonance of the embellishing tones (see **4.4** for a reminder on how to do this).
Replace and Restore: Replace the augmented triad in measure 3 with V^6/vi.
Transpose to D major.

132 The Supertonic Seventh Chord

10.13 Grieg: Lyric Piece, Op. 12, No. 3 ("The Watchman's Song"), 1–8

Highlight and Hear: Sing or bring out the tenor voice as you play. How does this experience influence your voicing (balance of the voices)?

Repeat and React: Use this method in the last two measures to hear the clash of anticipation in the upper voice. How might this affect your use of *rubato*?

Transpose to C major.

REPERTOIRE STUDY

The following two excerpts contain ii^7 chords, of course, but also many other patterns and harmonic issues studied in earlier chapters. Use all the analytical knowledge, reduction techniques, and expressive practice methods at your disposal to study, interpret, and memorize these passages. The suggestions are once again just a starting point.

10.14 Mendelssohn: Song Without Words, Op. 19, No. 1, 1–18

Suggested Practice Methods: Outer voices alone, block chord reduction in six voices, accompaniment alone without the melody and bass. All of these are excellent memory tests as well.

Analysis: Voice exchanges, cadences and modulation, secondary dominant chords, ii^7 chords.

Expression: Inflection of cadences, smooth connection of passing chords, dialog of outer voices.

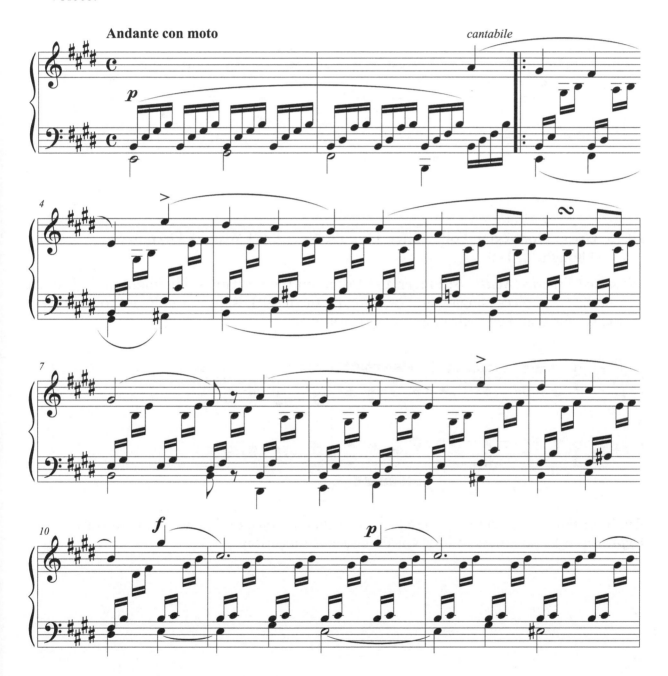

134 The Supertonic Seventh Chord

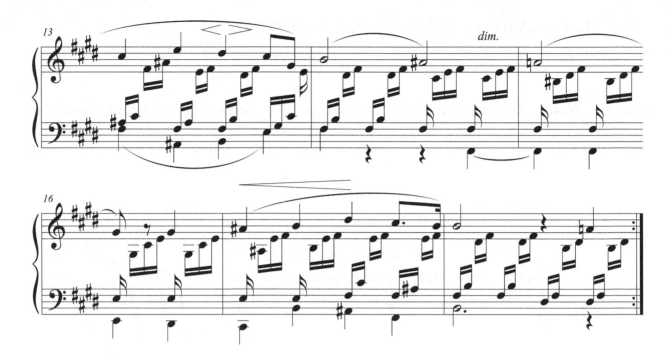

10.15 Grieg: Norwegian Folk Tunes, Op. 66, No. 18 ("I Wander Deep in Thought"), 1–9

Suggested Practice Methods: Linger and Listen on the tied notes, Highlight and Hear the middle two voices (singing and/or bringing them out), Repeat and React to hear all of the sevenths and embellishing tones, as follows:

Analysis: Find the ii^7 chords (there are six of them), voice exchanges, suspensions.
Expression: Dissonances in four voices, cadence inflection.

The Supertonic Seventh Chord   135

11 Sequences with Seventh Chords

In this chapter, we introduce the remaining diatonic seventh chords, which are used mainly in sequences. (The diminished and half-diminished seventh chords on the leading tone will be dealt with more fully in Chapters 12 and 14.) These major and minor seventh chords give added dissonance and color to the sequence of descending seconds (circle of fifths) that we studied in Chapter 3.

11.1 Bach: English Suite No. 3 in G Minor, Prelude, 67–88

In this excerpt, Bach establishes the key of B♭ major with seven measures of tonic and dominant harmony, then launches into a sequence of descending seconds that moves through the entire cycle of diatonic fifths from tonic to tonic (measures 74–81), and continues its downward momentum with a second complete sequence using a new pattern of figuration (measures 82–88). Both sequences alternate root position triads with diatonic major and minor seventh chords (shown by the figured bass).

11.2 Performance Considerations

As always, it is very useful to make a reduction of passages like the one above, so that we can hear the harmonies clearly, one next to the other, and compare their relative degrees of tension and release. Then, as we did in Chapter 3, we can put a + sign next to the chords that feel more active or tense. In this example, the preparation and resolution of the sevenths (marked with arrows and slurs below) suggests emphasizing the seventh chords slightly more than the triads (see + signs below), though an argument could be made for making the opposite inflection. Whatever one may decide, the important thing is to avoid giving each measure, and each chord, the same emphasis. Try playing this reduction with these different inflections, referring back also to the original score, to find out which interpretation you prefer.

GENERAL PRINCIPLES

11.3 Voice Leading and Variations

In the ii⁷–V⁷–I progression we studied in Chapter 10, the root motion of the three chords descends by fifths to the cadence (see **a.** below). In this chapter, we are essentially backing up this motion by fifths all the way to the tonic, to include seventh chords on IV, vii, iii, and vi (**b.**). The preparation of dissonance governing the voice leading of the ii⁷ chord applies to these chords as well: the seventh is prepared in the same voice and resolves down by step. In consecutive root position seventh chords, this creates alternating complete and incomplete chords (**b.** again).

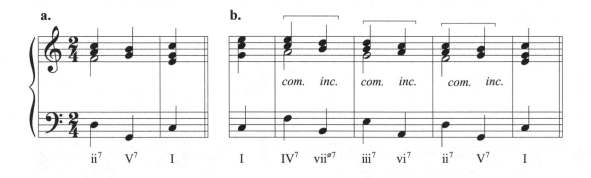

There are innumerable possibilities for varying this sequence: it can be used in both major and minor keys; the seventh chords may alternate with triads, as in the Bach example; all of the inversions may be used (see the sequences in **11.4**) as well as all three right-hand positions; the diatonic seventh chords may be interspersed with secondary dominant chords (**c.** below); or the sequence may be used to modulate (**d.**). When we add to this all the possibilities for varying the texture and the figuration, the possibilities are nearly endless, which is no doubt the reason this sequence has been used so extensively throughout the history of music.

EXERCISES

11.4 Model Sequences

The six sequences below are all variations of the same basic sequence: descending seconds with diatonic seventh chords. The other two main types of sequences (ascending seconds and descending thirds) are rarely used with diatonic seventh chords. Each sequence is given first in C major, then in A minor. Practice them as written, taking note of their patterns, then continue counterclockwise around the circle of fifths (F major, D minor, etc.). As you play, be aware which voice has the seventh (use Highlight and Hear to focus your attention on this) and feel the dissonance of the seventh against the root of the chord (intervals of a seventh or a second).

a. Root position 7th chords alternating with root position triads

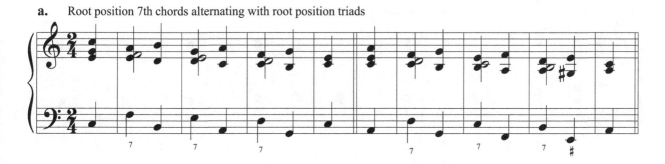

140 *Sequences with Seventh Chords*

b. All root position 7th chords

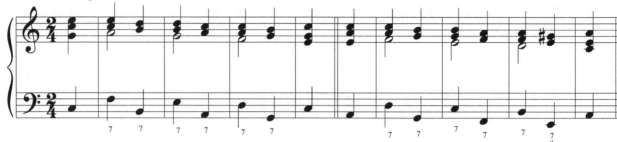

c. First inversion 7th chords alternating with root position triads

d. The same as c., in a different position

e. Third inversion 7th chords alternating with first inversion triads, in chorale style

f. Alternating first inversion and third inversion 7th chords, in chorale style

11.5 Handel: Lessons for Princess Anne, No. 12

This figured bass exercise is based almost entirely on sequences **c.** and **d.** in **11.4** above. It will be much easier if you practice those two sequences first in the keys of D minor, G minor, and A minor. Reducing the bass line to its essential notes is also helpful. Some soprano notes are suggested.

EXAMPLES

Play each of the examples below, then do the following:

- Make a block-chord reduction or continuo accompaniment.
- Put brackets over each unit of the sequence.
- Find the sevenths and mark their preparations with arrows, resolutions with slurs.
- Put figured bass numbers under the seventh chords (Roman numerals are unnecessary).
- Decide which of the two chords in the unit is more active and put a + by it.

- If some of the seventh chords are secondary dominants, identify them with Roman numerals.
- If the sequence modulates, indicate the change of key and pivot chord.
- Note any unusual or interesting features (rhythm, figuration, texture, etc.).

11.6 Bach: Partita No. 5 in G, Prelude, 5–18

Sequences with Seventh Chords 143

11.7 Bach: Prelude in C♯ Minor, *Well-Tempered Clavier*, Book 1, 1–8

11.8 Mozart: Piano Concerto in C, K. 503, III, 41–48

144 Sequences with Seventh Chords

11.9 Schubert: Impromptu in E♭, D. 899, No. 2, 25–35

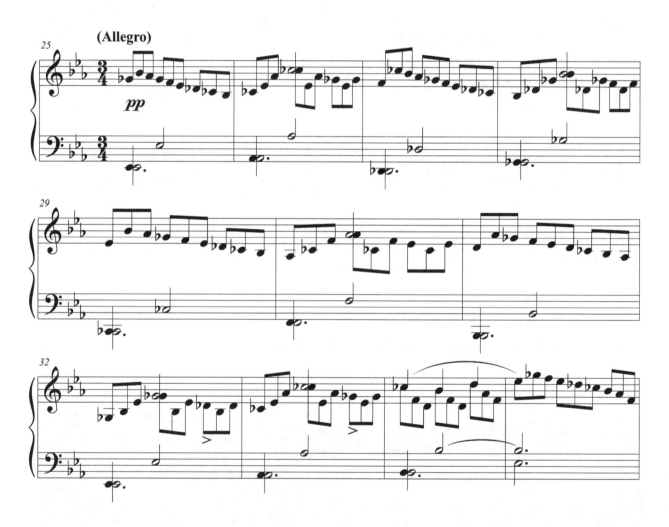

11.10 Schumann: *Kreisleriana*, Op. 16, No. 7, 9–22

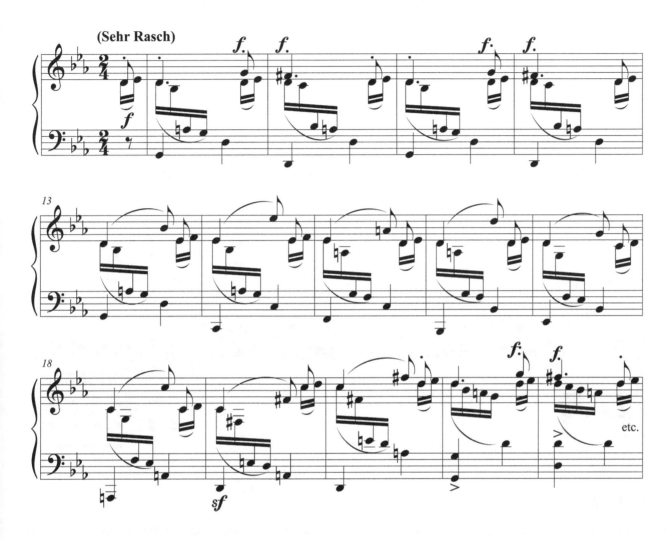

FILL-IN-THE-BLANK EXERCISES

11.11 Marcello, arr. Bach

Continue the sequential patterns in the left hand as indicated by the brackets.

146 Sequences with Seventh Chords

11.12 Mozart

Continue the three sequences as described. It helps to block the written patterns into chords first, then restore the figuration. You can also play a continuo accompaniment while someone else plays the original.

11.13 Grieg

Begin by blocking the chords and continuing the sequence as specified. Then play as written, repeating the entire eight measures two more times, each time an octave lower, and making a gradual *crescendo* as you descend. Add octaves to the left-hand melody the third time through. Note that the harmonic sequence follows the same pattern in each measure, but the rhythm of the melody changes from a two-measure pattern in the first line to a one-measure pattern in the second.

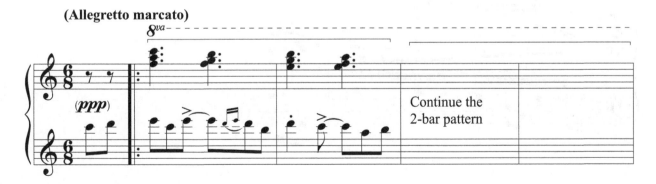

148 *Sequences with Seventh Chords*

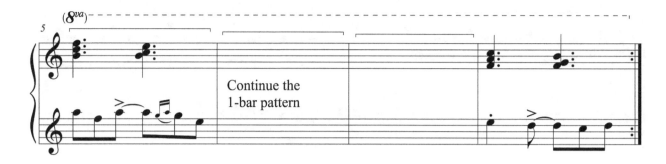

11.14 Medtner

Continue the left hand by following the instructions in the score (play the bass line by itself first, then block chords with two hands, then left hand alone as written), then add the right-hand melody.

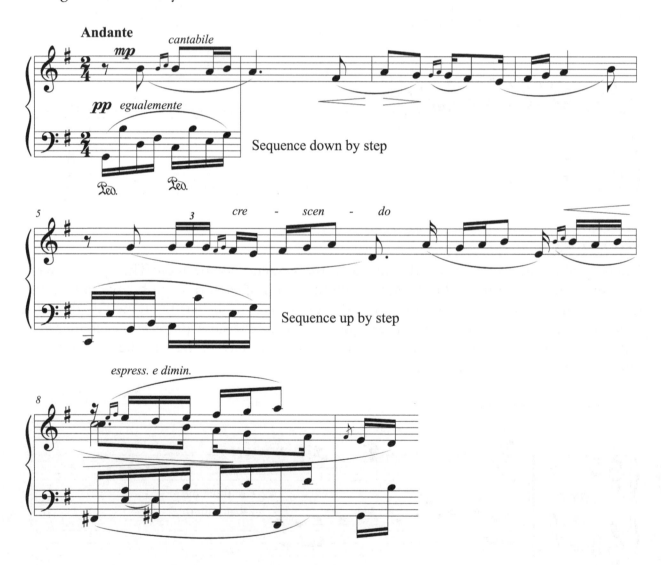

Sequences with Seventh Chords   149

REPERTOIRE STUDY

As in previous chapters, use the suggestions to learn, interpret and memorize the two excerpts below.

11.15 Johann Kuhnau: Prelude in G

Suggested Practice Method: Block chords.
Analysis: Modulations, sequences, secondary dominants, diatonic seventh chords, preparation and resolution of dissonances.
Expression: Add dynamics.

150 Sequences with Seventh Chords

11.16 Chopin: Ballade No. 1 in G Minor, Op. 23, 68–82

Suggested Practice Method: Outer voice reduction.

Analysis: Sequences, preparation and resolution of sevenths (particularly interesting in measures 72–75), secondary dominants, embellishing tones.

Expression: Pedaling, as it relates to harmony and embellishing tones (the pedal markings are Chopin's), inflection of harmony and embellishing tones.

Sequences with Seventh Chords   151

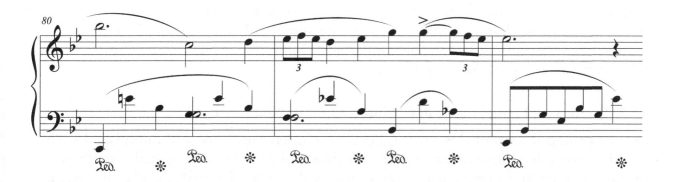

12 The Leading Tone Seventh Chord in Minor

The diminished seventh chord occurs diatonically on the seventh degree of the harmonic minor scale. In its diatonic form, which is the subject of this chapter, it functions as a dominant chord and resolves to the minor tonic. It also has a great many chromatic uses, which we will study in Chapters 13 and 17.

12.1 Beethoven: Piano Sonata in C Minor, Op. 10, No. 1, I, 1–22

In the opening section of this sonata, Beethoven alternates tonic and diminished seventh chords, saving the dominant seventh for the final cadence. The diminished seventh is used in root position and in two of its inversions, as shown in the analysis. Play the passage, noticing the smooth, stepwise connection of these chords to their resolutions.

Replace and Restore: To better appreciate the particular color of these diminished seventh chords, try replacing them with dominant chords. Simply lower the seventh of the chord—the A♭s in this example—a half step, to G. Then restore the diminished seventh chords and compare the difference.

DOI: 10.4324/9781003333289-13

GENERAL PRINCIPLES

12.2 Function

The vii°7 chord is built on the leading tone of the minor mode, and is made up entirely of minor thirds (**a.** below) It is sometimes considered a dominant ninth chord without the root (**b.**). The fact that the seventh of the chord frequently resolves down a half step to the fifth scale degree, creating a dominant seventh chord, is a further demonstration of its dominant function (**c.**). It can be used in all its inversions, although third inversion is rare (**d.**). The figured bass for the inversions sometimes looks complicated because of the alterations, but the chords themselves are easy to find on the keyboard since they are all constructed of only one interval—the minor third.

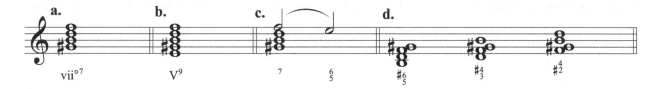

12.3 Relationship to V7

Since there is only one note's difference between vii°7 and V7, the easiest way to learn the voice leading of diminished seventh chords is to relate them to dominant sevenths. In the two progressions below, the dominant chords are changed to diminished simply by replacing the fifth scale degree (E) with the sixth (F). The resolutions remain the same. Notice, however, that the inversions change: first inversion dominant becomes root position diminished, second inversion becomes first inversion, and third inversion becomes second inversion. More importantly, the diminished chords retain the same neighbor and passing qualities as their dominant counterparts.

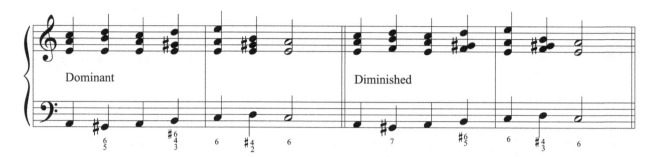

12.4 Resolutions

The standard resolutions of vii°7 are given below in all three right-hand positions, and in all the inversions except third, which is infrequently used. Compare them to V7 resolutions by replacing the sixth scale degree (F) with the fifth (E). Memorize these resolutions and try them in a few other minor keys. You can also convert them to chorale style by moving the alto down an octave and adjusting the bass where necessary.

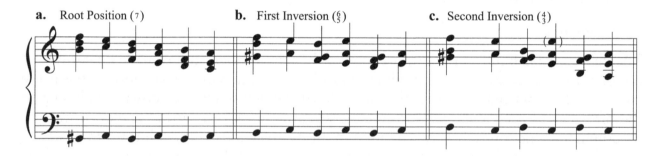

Progression **d.** shows some of the other resolutions of vii°7: voice exchanges that produce passing chords of different kinds, a sort of deceptive resolution to VI, and a parallel chromatic movement from vii°$^4_3$ to vii°7/V. Transpose this progression to a few other minor keys.

EXERCISES

12.5 Figured Bass

Practice these figured basses first with the left hand alone, just to find the chords (see **10.6** for a reminder on how to do this), then play in keyboard style, then chorale style. Starting positions are suggested, but others can also be used.

EXAMPLES

12.6 Haydn: Piano Sonata in E Minor, Hob. XVI:34, I, 81–87

Reduction: Play the excerpt as written, then make an outer voice reduction.
Analysis: Analyze the diminished seventh chord in the first line and the sequence in the second line.
Transposition: Transpose to G major (the key in which this passage first appears, in the exposition), replacing the diminished chord in the second measure with a dominant chord. You can read the right hand in the bass clef, two octaves higher, to help with this transposition. Compare your transposition to Haydn's original (measures 16–22), which is slightly different.

12.7 Mozart: Piano Concerto in D Minor, K. 466, III, 271–281

Analysis: Find the diminished seventh chords and the embellishing tones in the second line.

Expression: Add dynamic nuances to show how you would inflect the harmony.

Transposition: Transpose to F minor (not F major, as one might expect), imagining the right hand in the bass clef, two octaves higher. Notice that the C♯s become E♮s in F minor. Compare your transposition to measures 92–102 in Mozart's original, which as in the Haydn above, is not an identical transposition.

12.8 Beethoven: Piano Sonata in D, Op. 10, No. 3, II, 1–9

Analysis: Analyze all the chords, including the "other" resolutions of vii°⁷ (see **12.4d.**).

Repeat and React: Repeat the chords in measures 1–2 and 6 to fully appreciate the dissonance of the lower neighbor tones.

Reduction: Reduce the passage to its essential chords, leaving out the embellishing tones. Notice the voice exchanges and changing number of notes per chord and memorize this reduction.

Transposition: Transpose to F minor. Notice that all of the sharps become natural in the new key, with the exception of the D♯s in measure 6.

12.9 Schubert: Moment Musical, D. 780, No. 4, 1–8

Reduction: Reduce the passage to five-note blocked chords, listening to the soprano line that emerges from the figuration.

Analysis: Find the sevenths of all the seventh chords. Mark the preparation notes with arrows and draw slurs from the sevenths to their resolutions. Measure 7 is a Neapolitan sixth chord (see Chapter 15) preceded by a double suspension.

Expression: Add dynamic nuances based on your analysis of the preparation and resolution of the dissonances.

Transposition: Transpose to E minor, first in reduction, then restoring the figuration.

158 The Leading Tone Seventh Chord in Minor

12.10 Chopin: Etude, Op. 10, No. 4, 63–71

Reduction: Reduce the bass line to its main notes and play a keyboard style reduction.
Analysis: Analyze the voice exchanges, diminished seventh chords (including "other" resolutions), secondary dominants. Memorize the reduction using your understanding of the patterns.

12.11 Figured Bass Reconstructions

Melodies are usually easy to remember because we sing them to ourselves inwardly. Harmony is more difficult to memorize because it requires conceptualization (analysis) and hearing in multiple parts. That is why memory slips usually occur in the left hand, where harmony is normally situated in piano music. To help you memorize more analytically, the preceding three examples have been reduced to figured bass lines below. Try to reconstruct these passages, first in reduction, then as written, relying only on the bass lines and your aural and analytical memory. Afterwards, look back to the originals to check any details you may be unsure of.

REPERTOIRE STUDY

12.12 Chopin: Waltz in A Minor, Op. 34, No. 2, 17–36

Suggested Practice Methods: Melody as written with bass line (downbeat notes only) to hear how the rising bass line guides the phrase, left-hand accompaniment blocked with two hands to feel the voice leading better.

Analysis: Diminished sevenths and their "deceptive" resolutions (replace with normal resolutions to appreciate the difference), secondary dominants, embellishing tones in both the melody and the accompaniment.

Expression: Consider the inflection and timing (*rubato*) of the embellishing tones, particularly the neighbor tones followed by rests (remove the rests to compare the difference) and the suspensions in the left hand. Also consider the overall arc of each phrase (where are the climaxes?).

12.13 Schumann: Carnaval, Op. 9, *Chiarina*, 1–16

Suggested Practice Methods: Left-hand accompaniment blocked with two hands, noticing the changes between the first phrase and the second; right hand reduced to two main notes per measure (remove suspensions) together with the bass line, noticing parallel motion between middle voice and bass, and contrary motion (with voice exchange) of the upper part.

Analysis: Diminished sevenths and their resolutions, cadences, embellishing tones.

Expression: Pedaling as related to your understanding of the harmony and embellishing tones.

13 Secondary Diminished Chords

Like their close cousins the secondary dominant chords, secondary diminished chords add color and forward motion to harmonic progressions. Although the diminished seventh chord occurs diatonically in the minor mode, as we saw in Chapter 12, it is used in both major and minor modes as a secondary chord.

13.1 Schumann: Album for the Young, Op. 68, No. 20, 1–8

In this excerpt, Schumann uses the same four-measure melody two times, changing only the last note the second time. But whereas the harmony in the first phrase is entirely diatonic (including some very beautiful ii^7 chords), the second phrase adds four chromatic chords—all secondary diminished chords, as shown in the analysis. Notice that all of these chords fall on weak beats, or weak parts of beats, creating a sense of forward motion across the beats to their resolutions, and inviting a lingering *rubato* to underscore their expressiveness. The German performance instructions mean "slow and played with expression."

Replace and Restore: To better appreciate Schumann's lovely harmonies, try replacing the F in measure 3 with an F♯, turning the ii^7 chord into V/V (at least one older edition makes this spurious "correction"). Also try making the cadence at the end of the passage a conventional PAC in G major.

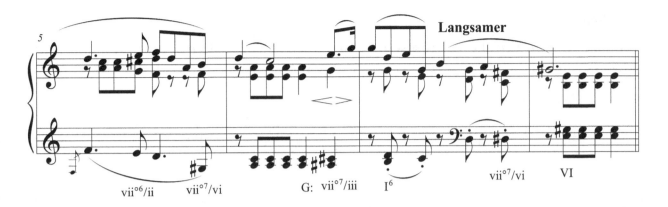

EXERCISES

13.2 Progressions

Secondary diminished chords often fill in gaps in the bass line between diatonic chords. When the gap in the bass line is an ascending whole step, the bass fills in a chromatic half step and supports a root position diminished chord (see **a.**, below). When the gap is a descending third, the bass fills in the scale and supports a second inversion diminished chord (**b.**).

You can get a sense of this "filling-in" phenomenon by leaving the diminished chords out of these two progressions. When you then add them back in, you can feel how these chords create forward motion toward their resolutions. As always, transpose these progressions to a few different keys. You can also play them in chorale style by moving the alto voice an octave lower (adjusting the octave of the bass note if the stretch becomes too large).

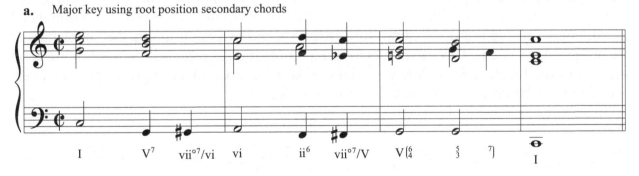

13.3 Sequences

Secondary diminished chords are also used in sequences, most often in the descending thirds sequence, and in the major mode. Transpose these two sequences to a few different keys.

a. Descending thirds with root position secondary chords

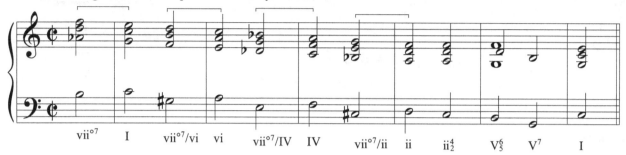

b. Descending thirds with second inversion secondary chords

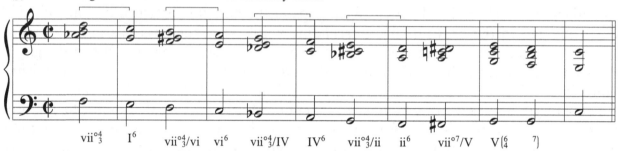

13.4 Figured Bass

In the figured basses below, the secondary diminished chords are missing. You can find them by filling in the gaps in the bass line and building up minor thirds on the added bass note. When the gap to be filled in is an ascending second, use a root position diminished chord; when the gap is a descending third, use a second inversion diminished chord (as in the progressions in **13.2**). Write the missing bass note in the staff and the Roman numeral analysis in the blank space below it. Suggested starting positions are given for each exercise. They can be done in keyboard or chorale style.

EXAMPLES

13.5 Mozart: Piano Sonata in D, K. 311, II, 65–74

This is a good example of a bass descending by thirds, filled in with passing diminished seventh chords (and one dominant seventh). Leave out these passing chords to uncover the fundamental progression, then add them back in. Analyze the embellishing tones, notice the differences between the first phrase and the second, then try to play the excerpt from memory.

13.6 Beethoven: Variations on the Russian Dance from *Das Waldmächen*, WoO 71, Var. 3, 1–10

In this example, the diminished seventh chords fall on the beats rather than in between them, creating an inflection similar to accented neighbor tones. Once again, practice leaving them out to reveal the essential progression, notice the difference between the first phrase and the second, and memorize.

166 *Secondary Diminished Chords*

13.7 Beethoven: Piano Concerto No. 4, Op. 58, III, 280–287

This example features a rather unusual rising sequence. The accidentals make it somewhat difficult to sight-read, but once you figure out the pattern, it becomes easier. Practice in block chords, then leave out the diminished seventh chords to reveal the overall pattern.

13.8 Figured Bass Reconstructions

Below, the three preceding examples have been reduced to their fundamental bass lines, with the diminished seventh chords removed. Test your memory of these passages by reconstructing them from the figured bass, first without the diminished sevenths and embellishing material, then as written. Consult the originals for any details you may have forgotten, then play them again from memory.

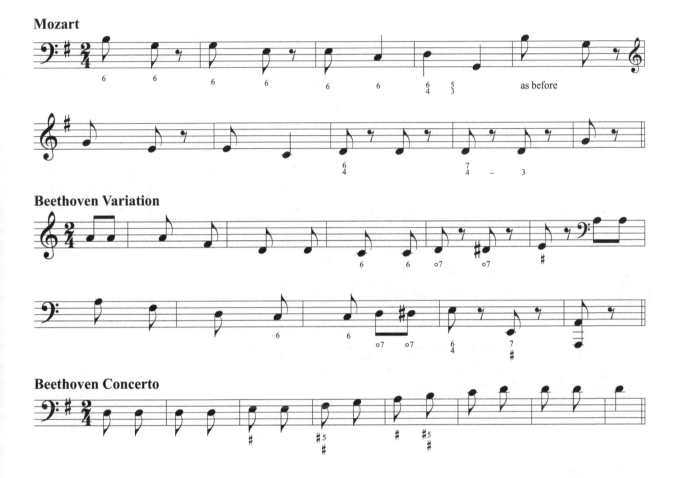

Mozart

Beethoven Variation

Beethoven Concerto

FILL-IN-THE-BLANK EXERCISES

13.9 Schumann

In this excerpt, the middle voices in the right hand have been removed after the first measure. Play it through once as written, with just the outer voices, imagining the chords suggested by these outer voices. Then play it a second time, instinctively adding what you imagine to be missing in the inner voices. Finally, try it a third time, using the figured bass to help you figure out any chords you were unsure of. The German performance instructions mean, roughly, "slower and haltingly (or hesitantly)." Identify the cadences, keys, secondary diminished chords, and voice exchanges.

168 Secondary Diminished Chords

13.10 Schubert

In this excerpt, the sixteenth-note inner line has been removed after the first four measures. Continue it in a similar manner, feeling free to make the line more florid when the melody moves in slower rhythmic values, as Schubert does in measures 3–4. It helps to play a block chord version first, before breaking the inner voices up into sixteenth notes. Identify the secondary chords.

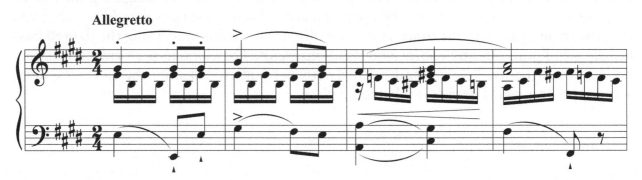

MELODY HARMONIZATIONS

Because of their complexity, the following four melodies have been annotated with symbols and instructions of different kinds that will help you to reconstruct the composers' harmonizations. These annotations constitute a sort of analytical narration of what is happening in the music. This kind of narration, whether written or spoken (aloud or in our minds) can become a powerful aid to concentration, helping us to think the music as we play.

13.11 Schubert

Add a spread position accompaniment, practicing it first with two hands to find good voice leading. Note the beautiful embellishing tones on the first beats of nearly every measure (the first two are indicated).

170 *Secondary Diminished Chords*

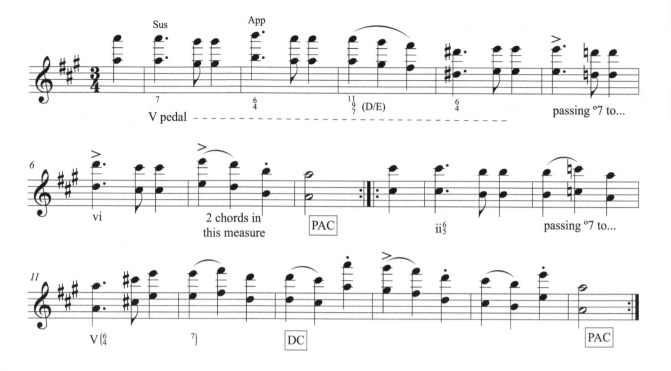

13.12 Chopin

Start by finding the bass line and playing that together with the upper-voice melody (the dotted quarter notes), then with the complete right hand, listening for the dissonance of the lower neighbor tones in the eighth-note pattern. Then practice the accompaniment by itself, again in spread position, first with two hands, then with the left hand alone, before putting the hands together.

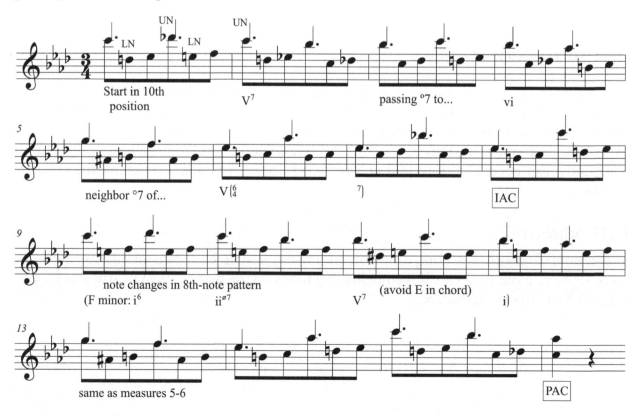

13.13 Schumann

Once again, find the bass line first, then work out the chords, blocking them with two hands. The diminished seventh chords in this excerpt are inverted, but since this chord is made up of minor thirds in all its inversions, the simpler symbol °7 is used rather than the inversion figures. When the chords change twice per measure, the accompaniment pattern should be altered to go up on each chord, rather than up, then down.

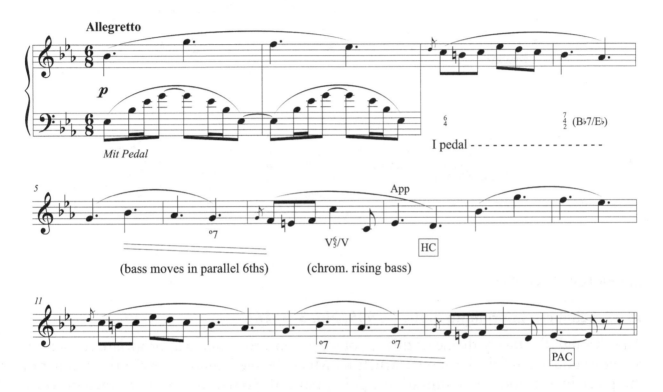

13.14 Beethoven: Piano Sonata in C Minor, Op. 13, I, 1–11

If you've already played this famous movement, you can use these annotations as a model for the kind of detailed mental narrative you can make of the music you play. If you have not yet played this piece, you should be able to reconstruct it fairly accurately just by following the annotations. Afterwards, check your accuracy by consulting the original score.

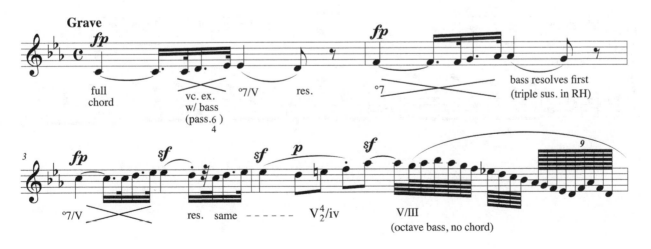

172 *Secondary Diminished Chords*

REPERTOIRE STUDY

13.15 Schubert: Impromptu in B♭, D. 935, No. 3, 1–16

Play through the lovely theme of this set of variations, then make appropriate reductions to better understand the harmonic structure. Make detailed annotations in the manner of the preceding melody harmonizations, going beyond Roman numerals to include voice leading patterns, cadences, modulations, expressive embellishing tones, and anything else that seems interesting to you. Speak this analytical narrative out loud as you play, first with the score, then without it. If there are still gray areas in your memory, try to find another way to explain those passages to yourself.

Secondary Diminished Chords 173

14 The Leading Tone Seventh Chord in Major

In the major mode, the seventh chord built on the leading tone is half-diminished in quality. Like its near relation the fully diminished seventh chord on the leading tone of the minor mode, it functions as a replacement for the dominant seventh. It is also used as a secondary chord of the dominant.

14.1 Schubert: Piano Sonata in A Minor, D. 845, II, 1–15

At the beginning of this movement, after a five-measure phrase in A minor, Schubert modulates to C major in the second phrase, whose climactic chord is the half-diminished seventh chord built on the leading tone of that key (indicated by its Roman numeral).

Replace and Restore: Replace the As in this chord with Gs to hear the difference between the half-diminished seventh chord and the dominant seventh. The function is the same, but the color is different.

GENERAL PRINCIPLES

14.2 Primary Use

The vii⁰⁷ chord is called half-diminished because while the fifth of the chord is diminished, the seventh is minor (that is to say, undiminished—see **a.**, below). Like its fully diminished relative, it is sometimes considered a dominant ninth chord without the root (**b.**). It is closely related to V^6_5, which can be obtained simply by lowering the seventh of the chord a step (**c.**). The chord can be used in all its inversions, though third inversion is rare (**d.**).

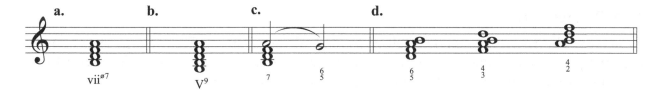

Composers often use vii⁰⁷ in order to have an upper neighbor motion ($\hat{6}$-$\hat{5}$) in the melody, rather than the common note that V^6_5 produces when it resolves to I (compare **a.** to **b.**, below). For this reason, the seventh of the chord is almost always in the soprano. In order to avoid parallel fifths, the tonic chord to which vii⁰7 resolves must double the third rather than the root (**b.**). Both the first and second inversions of vii⁰⁷ resolve to I⁶, again usually with the seventh in the soprano, and with a doubled third in the resolution chord (**c.** and **d.**).

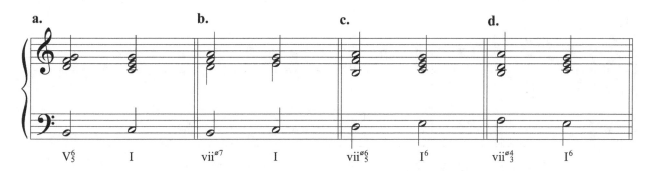

14.3 Secondary Use

The half-diminished seventh chord is more often used as a secondary chord of the dominant, normally connecting either IV or ii$^6_5$ to the cadential $^6_4$ chord (**a.** and **b.**, below). This is a very smooth connection, with the bass simply filling in the whole step between $\hat{4}$ and $\hat{5}$ with a chromatic passing tone, while one of the upper voices anticipates the third of the I$^6_4$ chord.

176 *The Leading Tone Seventh Chord in Major*

14.4 Progressions

Transpose the two progressions below to several major keys. The first progression (**a.**) uses the primary vii°7 chord in root position, first and second inversion. The second progression (**b.**) uses the vii°7/V in two different right-hand positions.

EXAMPLES

14.5 Schubert: Moment Musical, D. 780, No. 6, 1–16

Reduction: Outer voices, listening for dissonances.
Analysis: Suspensions in measures 1, 3, etc.; the vii°7 chord; compare measures 2–4 with 10–12.
Expression: Observe the changing number of voices (from 4 to 7) and its effect on voicing and dynamics.

* French augmented 6th chord (see chapter 16)

14.6 Schumann: *Der Dichter spricht* ("The Poet Speaks"), *Kinderszenen*, Op. 15, No. 13, 14–26

Highlight and Hear: Sing the tenor voice, listening for the dissonances in measures 16–17. Where does the G♯ in measure 19 resolve?
Analysis: Keys and cadences, diminished and half-diminished chords.
Expression: Effect of rests and syncopations in the second line.

MELODY HARMONIZATIONS

14.7 Schubert

Add a spread position left-hand accompaniment. The harmony contains both half-diminished and fully diminished secondary chords, as shown by the Roman numerals.

14.8 Schubert

Continue the left-hand accompaniment in the manner of the first measure. Most measures have two chords per measure. Finding the bass line first, without the offbeat chords, will make it easier.

The Leading Tone Seventh Chord in Major 179

REPERTOIRE STUDY

14.9 Mendelssohn: Variations, Op. 82, Theme

Reduction: Outer voices.

Analysis: Keys and cadences, half-diminished chords (used both as vii°7 and ii°7), voice exchanges, deceptive resolutions, secondary chords, suspensions. Using all this information, construct an analytical narrative (as in Chapter 13) that you can speak to yourself as you play the excerpt.

Expression: Effect of rising bass line on phrase inflection, cadence inflection, suspension preparation, effect of texture (number of voices) on dynamics.

180 The Leading Tone Seventh Chord in Major

14.10 Grieg: Lyric Piece, Op. 43, No. 1 ("Butterfly"), 1–6

Reduction: Blocked (or rolled) chords in five or six voices.
Analysis: vii°7 chords, embellishing vii°7 chords, key change, "twist" on resolution of cadential $^6_4$ in measures 5–6.
Note: The next section of this piece is shown in **15.13**.

The Leading Tone Seventh Chord in Major

15 The Neapolitan Sixth Chord

The Neapolitan sixth chord, also analyzed as bII⁶, is a chromatic substitute for the iv or ii°⁶ chord in the minor mode. Its unique color is easy to recognize and, although it is a major triad, it lends a somewhat dark expressive hue to the harmonic palette.

15.1 Mozart: Piano Concerto in A, K. 488, II, 1–12

The opening solo of this movement contains myriad beauties, but one of the most striking is the Neapolitan sixth chord near the end. It is a simple G-major triad, but in the context of the F#-minor tonality, its color is so special that Mozart lingers over it for two measures before continuing to the cadence.

DOI: 10.4324/9781003333289-16

The Neapolitan Sixth Chord 183

GENERAL PRINCIPLES

15.2 Function and Doubling

The close relationship of N⁶ to iv and ii°⁶ is easy to see in the following progression. We give these chords three different labels, but in reality ii°⁶ and N⁶ are simply variants of the iv chord (pre-dominant function). As with ii°⁶, the root of N⁶ is usually in the soprano, and the third of the chord (the bass note) is normally doubled.

15.3 Progressions

In the simplest progression (**a.**, below), the N⁶ chord can be approached directly from the tonic chord and proceed directly to the dominant. It is also frequently preceded by VI (as in the Mozart example above), and followed by vii°⁷/V (**b.**). Practice these two progressions in several minor keys.

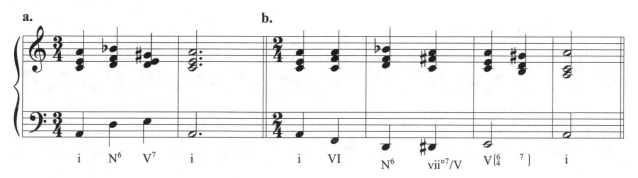

15.4 Drill: Finding N⁶

Practice this drill until you can find the chords easily.

1. Choose a minor key.
2. Name the Neapolitan chord in that key. Just think of the major triad a half step above the tonic.
3. Play the N⁶ in first inversion. The left hand plays $\hat{4}$ and the right hand plays the triad in sixth shape with the root ($\flat\hat{2}$) in the soprano.
4. Play an incomplete V⁷ with $\hat{7}$ in the soprano.
5. Resolve to i.
6. Embellish the progression with extra chords as in **15.3b**.

EXAMPLES

Play the following three examples, reduce them to their essential chords and analyze them, then reconstruct them and transpose them using the figured basses in **15.8**.

15.5 Bach, arr. Stradal: Adagio from Organ Sonata No. 4, 1–3

Compare the progression in this excerpt to the sequence in **3.4b** (minor version).

15.6 Beethoven: Piano Sonata in C♯ Minor, Op. 27, No. 2, I, 1–5

Replace and Restore: To better appreciate the particular color of the N⁶ chord, try replacing it with a iv chord.

15.7 Mendelssohn: Song Without Words, Op. 102, No. 4, 3–7

Compare the progression in this excerpt to the one in **15.5**.

15.8 Figured Bass Reconstructions

Below, the three preceding examples are reduced to figured bass lines. Add right-hand chords in keyboard style, then try to remember the figuration from the original and restore that. Transpose the bass, then the simple chords, then the figuration, up a fourth, then down a fourth.

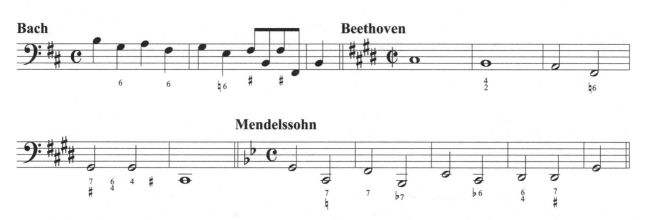

186 *The Neapolitan Sixth Chord*

MELODY HARMONIZATIONS

15.9 Beethoven

Add a waltz accompaniment using two notes rather than three for the chords on the second and third beats. Transpose to D minor and E minor, transposing the melody first before adding the accompaniment.

15.10 Chopin

Add a waltz accompaniment. Two of the four phrases end in deceptive cadences. There are three N^6 chords, two of which should be obvious from the accidentals. The last phrase is simply a prolonged PAC with a cadential $^6_4$. Transpose to D minor and E minor.

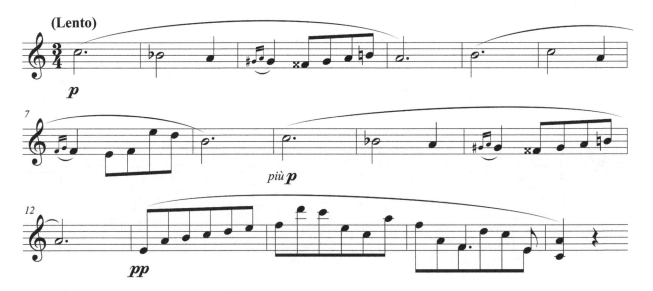

15.11 Chopin

Once again, add a spread position waltz accompaniment. The first melody note adds a poignant minor ninth to the V⁷ chord. Some of the embellishing tones have been labeled to make it easier to find the chords.

REPERTOIRE STUDY

15.12 Chopin: Etude, Op. 10, No. 6, 1–16

Reduction: Analyze the pattern of the embellishing tones in the sixteenth-note line, then reduce it to its main notes and play a four-voice chorale style reduction. If you write down your reduction, you can use it as a memory aid (try to play the complete score from the reduction).

Analysis: Make a complete harmonic analysis, including the Neapolitan chord.

Expression: From the reduction, find the overarching inflection of the eight-measure phrase. Use Repeat and React or Linger and Listen to become aware of the acute dissonance of some of the sixteenth notes in the tenor voice.

188 *The Neapolitan Sixth Chord*

15.13 Grieg: Lyric Piece, Op. 43, No. 1 ("Butterfly"), 7–17

Reduction: Play the melody and bass together (**a.** below), then reduce the harmony to its main chords (**b.**). These two reductions can also be combined and the figuration gradually restored.

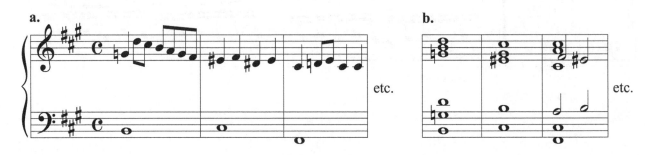

Analysis: Keys, Neapolitan chords, embellishing chords.

Note: The first section of this piece is shown in **14.10**. These two excerpts together comprise almost the entire piece, which could therefore be completed quite quickly.

190 *The Neapolitan Sixth Chord*

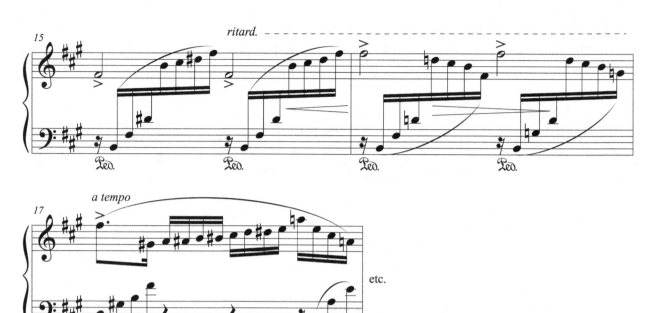

16 Augmented Sixth Chords

Augmented sixth chords are a set of pre-dominant chords that arise from chromatic motion toward the dominant. They often fill in the gaps between diatonic chords, creating a heightened sense of tension and movement. In this chapter, we study the three "nationalities" of augmented sixth chords and their standard resolutions. In Chapter 17, we will look at some of the other, less standard, ways of using them.

16.1 Mozart: Piano Sonata in D, K. 284, III, Var. VII

In this variation, Mozart uses three augmented sixth (+6) chords in three very different ways. The first one, an Italian +6, comes at the climax of the first phrase and is a result of the chromatic filling-in of both the bass line and the upper voice, moving in contrary motion to each other. The harmonic rhythm is rapid here, helping to create a drive to the half cadence. In the second phrase, a German +6 helps to move the music forward, this time towards a PAC in the key of A minor, and with a harmonic rhythm that is more spread out, with the D-minor chord in measure 5 (iv^6 in the new key) and its transformation into the augmented sixth taking up two full measures before culminating on a cadential $^6_4$ chord. The third phrase contains no augmented sixth chords, but does have two other chromatic chords that you should recognize. The last phrase again uses an Italian +6 at the climax, but this time it is approached by a rising bass line, uses only three notes, falls exceptionally on a strong beat, and continues into a PAC in the home key.

192 *Augmented Sixth Chords*

GENERAL PRINCIPLES

16.2 Types of Augmented Sixth Chords

Augmented sixth chords are built on the note a half step above the dominant—diatonic $\hat{6}$ in the minor mode, lowered $\hat{6}$ in major. Above this bass note, the raised fourth scale degree ($\sharp\hat{4}$) is added, creating the interval for which these chords are named—an augmented sixth (**a.**, below). Adding the tonic scale degree to these two notes gives us the Italian +6 (**b.**). Adding $\hat{2}$ to the Italian chord makes it French (**c.**); adding $\hat{3}$ makes it German (**d.**). Note: The French chord is sometimes given the figured bass $\frac{4}{3}$ and the German chord $\frac{6}{5}$, but this seems unnecessary since their names already distinguish them from each other.

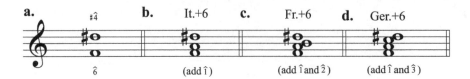

16.3 Resolutions

In all three of the augmented sixth chords, the interval of the augmented sixth resolves outward to an octave of the dominant ($\hat{6} \to \hat{5}$, $\sharp\hat{4} \to \hat{5}$). The Italian chord can be in three voices, or in four with $\hat{1}$ doubled. The German chord usually resolves first to the cadential $^6_4$, avoiding the parallel fifths that would result from resolving directly to V. All three chords can occur in any position of the upper voices, as illustrated below, but they are rarely inverted. (See, however, the exception in **16.5g**.) Practice the resolutions below in a few different minor keys.

EXERCISES

16.4 Drill: Finding the Augmented Sixth Chords

This drill will help you to find the augmented sixth chords without the help of notation.

1. Choose a minor key.
2. Find the fifth scale degree in both hands, two octaves apart.
3. From that note, move the left hand up a half step to $\hat{6}$ and the right hand down a half step to $\sharp\hat{4}$. Name these two notes, which form the interval of the augmented sixth.
4. Add the tonic scale degree to the right hand. You now have a three-note Italian +6.
5. Resolve to the dominant triad, then to the tonic.
6. To play the Italian chord in four voices, add another tonic scale degree (at the octave or the unison).
7. To make a French +6 chord, add $\hat{2}$ to the three-note Italian chord. Resolve to the dominant triad or to a cadential $^6_4$.
8. To make a German chord, add $\hat{3}$ to the three-note Italian chord. You can also think of a dominant seventh chord built on the bass note, and re-spell it mentally as an augmented sixth. Resolve to a cadential $^6_4$ before going to V.
9. Try all of these chords in different keys and different positions, in keyboard and chorale style.

16.5 Progressions

These progressions illustrate some of the most common approaches to the augmented sixth chord. To appreciate their "filling-in" character, try leaving out the augmented sixth chords,

194 *Augmented Sixth Chords*

then adding them back in. As you play, feel how the chromaticism intensifies the pre-dominant harmony in its movement towards the dominant. Two of these progressions require additional explanation: in **f.**, the German chord is enharmonically re-spelled (D♯ instead of E♭) when it resolves to the major $^6_4$; in **g.**, the German chord has ♯4 in the bass rather than $\hat{6}$, changing the interval of the augmented sixth to its inversion, the diminished third. Transpose these progressions to several other keys. You can also convert them to chorale style by moving the alto an octave lower and adjusting the octave of the bass where necessary, or simply by playing as written, but taking the tenor voice with the left hand instead of with the right.

16.6 Figured Bass

In these figured basses, blank spaces have been left where augmented sixth chords should be filled in. Write the bass note in the staff and the name of the augmented sixth chord that best fits the progression in the blank space below. Starting positions have been suggested, but as always, it is instructive to try other positions as well.

EXAMPLES

16.7 Beethoven: Bagatelle, Op. 33, No. 4, 17–30

Play this excerpt through in block chords, taking conscious note of all the chords and voice leading patterns you now recognize, and speaking your analysis out loud as you play. Then play the passage as written, and finally, a third time trying to look mainly at the bass line, glancing at the upper staff only when needed.

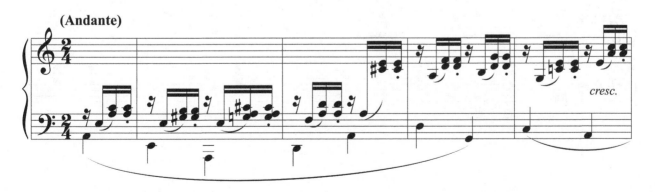

16.8 Chopin: Mazurka, Op. 63, No. 3, 57–64

Play the melody with only the bass line (no chords), then the accompaniment in block chords with two hands, then as written, speaking the analysis as you play. Note the expressive and unusual embellishing tones, as well as the sped-up harmonic rhythm in measures 61–62 (a hemiola).

16.9 Chopin: Etude, Op. 10, No. 3, 14–21

Reduce the bass line to its fundamental notes (one or two per measure) and notice its mirror-like symmetry (like a palindrome). Play the melody with this bass line, then play a block chord reduction, speaking the analysis as you play. Finally, play as written.

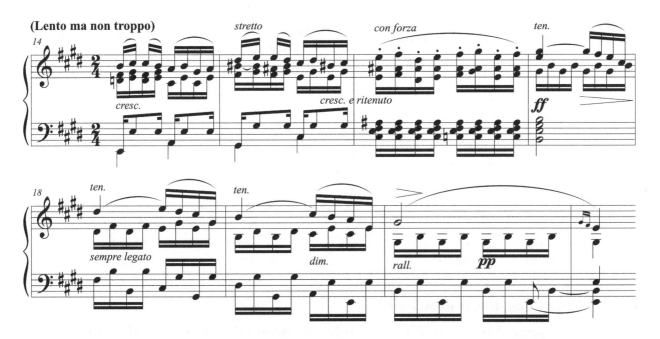

16.10 Chopin: Impromptu No. 1, Op. 29, 1–8

Play the bass line in half notes, noticing the two places where the same note carries over the bar line (syncopations). Add the melody (as written or reduced) to this bass line and feel how the bass guides the phrase. Reduce the left hand to three-four note block chords and play it with two hands, speaking the analysis as you play. Include the modulation and spelling of the augmented sixth chord in your analysis.

198 Augmented Sixth Chords

16.11 Figured Bass Reconstructions

Realize these figured basses first with simple chords in keyboard style, then use them to reconstruct the original excerpts above, going through the same reductions you made with each example (outer voices, block chords, etc.). In addition to the figured bass, a few annotations have been added to help you remember the originals.

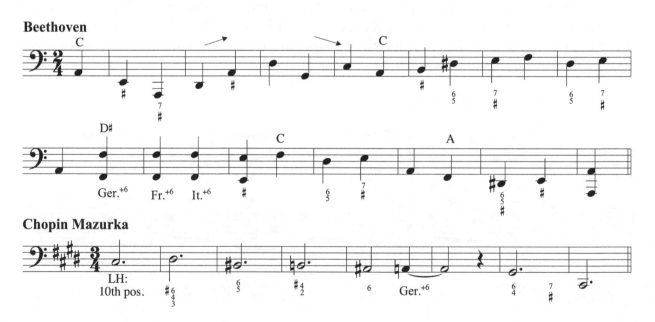

Chopin Etude

Chopin Impromptu

MELODY HARMONIZATIONS

16.12 Czerny

Add an accompaniment in close position using a flowing eighth-note rhythm. The B♭s clearly suggest N⁶ chords. There are no accidentals to help you find the two +6 chords Czerny uses, but remember that these chords precede the dominant.

16.13 Schubert

Add an accompaniment in spread position. The placement of the +6 chord should be clear from the accidental.

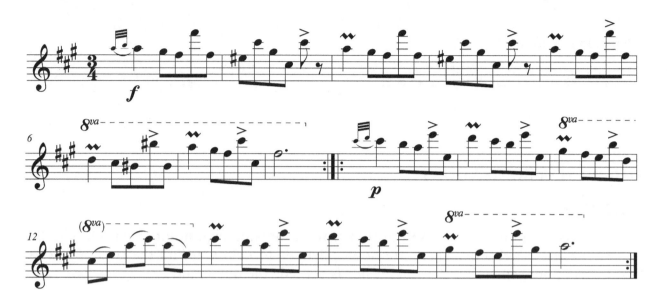

16.14 Schubert

Add a bass chord accompaniment in spread position. Look for a bass line that descends by step through the first six measures of the second half.

16.15 Schumann

Add a waltz accompaniment.

16.16 Chopin

Add a spread position accompaniment in flowing eighth notes. The bass line has been given to help you find the chords. Identify all four of the chromatic chords.

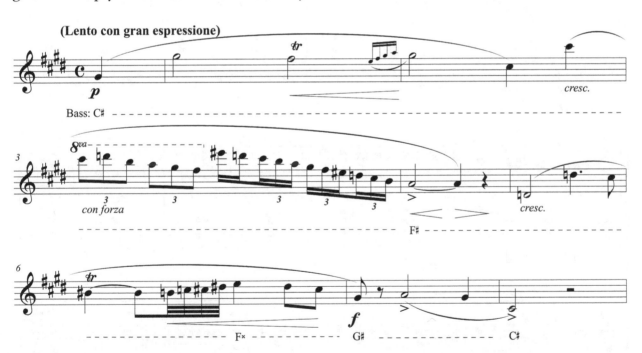

REPERTOIRE STUDY

16.17 Rachmaninoff: Nocturne, Op. 10, No. 1, 1–17

Suggested Practice Methods:

- Melody with bass line (how does the bass guide the phrase?).
- Accompaniment in block chords with two hands (note any irregularities in the voice leading).
- Linger and Listen, especially on tied notes and longer melodic notes.
- Highlight and Hear, especially on the inner voice beginning in measure 8, and on the bass line.

Analysis:

- Augmented sixth and other chromatic chords.
- Important embellishing tones.
- Compare measures 1–8 with 9–17.

17   Chromatic Voice Leading Techniques

Some chord progressions are derived from linear chromatic voice leading, and cannot be meaningfully analyzed using conventional Roman numeral analysis. There are an unlimited number of ways to connect chords chromatically; in this chapter we look at three of the most common ones: chromatic neighbor chords, omnibus progressions, and enharmonic re-spelling. Because chromatic harmony can be difficult to read, and hard to memorize, we will introduce some ways of thinking and practicing that should help to make such passages easier to assimilate.

17.1 Liszt: *Funérailles, Harmonies poétiques et religieuses*, No. 7, 56–64

Before trying to analyze this passage, play it through first, enjoying the plaintive melody and sumptuous harmony.

While the melancholy beauty of this passage is easy to appreciate, the chromatic harmony is difficult to describe in conventional terms. Even if we could find Roman numerals for

DOI: 10.4324/9781003333289-18

the second chord in the first measure, or for the progression in measures 60–61, they would do little to explain the logic of the passage, or help us to memorize it. But if we play the spread position accompaniment in block chords with two hands, as we have done so often in this book, the linear logic becomes apparent. The second chord is a chromatic neighbor chord on the tonic pedal, and the progression in the second line is a sequential pattern built on a descending chromatic bass.

At the same time, the mind likes to give names to individual chords. We naturally recognize the second chord as a diminished seventh, and the chords in the descending passage likewise have identifiable qualities. Rather than trying to force Roman numerals upon these chords, we can use a more informal method that labels them with letter names, or pop symbols, as they are sometimes called. Difficult-to-read chords, like the second one in measure 60, can even be mentally re-spelled enharmonically (changing flats to sharps or *vice versa*) if that makes them easier to think.

Both of these ways of thinking—the horizontal and the vertical—are illustrated in the analysis below. The idea here is not to make a scholarly analysis, but to find a practical way of describing the music to ourselves that allows us to learn it and remember it easily. Try playing this reduction as you speak the descriptions, once for the horizontal thinking and once for the chord names, and you will probably find that you can play it from memory after that.

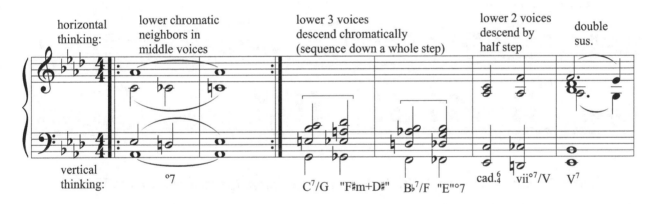

CHROMATIC NEIGHBOR CHORDS

17.2 Neighboring Diminished Seventh and Augmented Sixth Chords

We have already encountered diatonic neighbor chords—the neighbor $^6_4$, inversions of the V^7 chord that function as neighbor chords, etc.—elsewhere in this book. Here we add two chromatic neighbor chords: the neighboring diminished seventh and the neighboring augmented sixth, also known as common-tone chords because they share the same bass note as the tonic chord they embellish. The progressions below are given in both chorale style and in close position left-hand chords. Practice them both ways in a few different keys.

17.3 Chopin: Mazurka, Op. 67, No. 4, 1–8

Play the accompaniment with two hands, as in the Liszt analysis in **17.1**, and identify the chromatic neighbor chord. Note the unusual absence of the third in the tonic chord.

Replace and Restore: Replace the chromatic neighbor chord with a diatonic neighbor $^6_4$ and compare the difference.

17.4 Liszt: *Au lac de Wallenstadt, Années de pèlerinage (première année)*, 77–89

Simplify the left hand and play the right hand as written. Identify the chromatic neighbor chords and mentally re-spell them to make them easier to read.

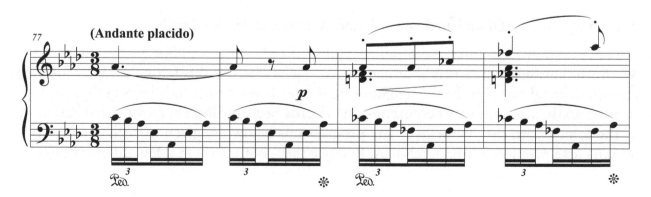

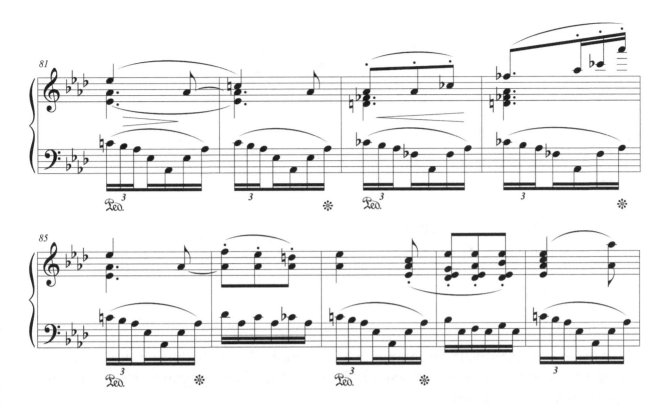

MELODY HARMONIZATIONS

17.5 Diabelli

Add a close position accompaniment in waltz style. Use chromatic neighbor chords on the accented notes, remembering to leave these melody notes out of the left-hand chords.

17.6 Tchaikovsky

Add a close position accompaniment in an offbeat eighth-note rhythm (eighth rest and eighth-note chord). The whole first line is on a tonic pedal. Use an augmented sixth chord before the half cadence. The last phrase modulates to the relative major.

17.7 Chopin

Add a spread position waltz accompaniment, using both a neighboring diminished seventh and a secondary diminished seventh. Note that the key signature reflects the key of the piece, not of this passage.

OMNIBUS PROGRESSIONS

17.8 Schubert: Piano Sonata in A Minor, D. 845, I, 34–40

The first two measures of this example feature another kind of chromatic neighbor chord. These *fz* chords happen to be spelled like dominant seventh chords, but they are decidedly not dominant in function (V^7/♭III?). When this chord is re-spelled at the end of the third measure and continues outward chromatically, it becomes part of a larger pattern known as an omnibus progression. Omnibus progressions are a kind of chromatic voice exchange, with two lines (the bass and an upper voice) moving in contrary motion to each other. Along the way, these diverging lines create other recognizable chords, but these are passing in nature, and serve to prolong the dominant chord, as shown in the analysis here.

17.9 The Extended Omnibus

The omnibus progression can be extended to a full octave of the chromatic bass line, as shown in **a.**, below. Play this progression slowly, noticing the patterns, both in the horizontal direction (the voice exchanges) and the vertical (the types of chords produced, as indicated by the figured bass). Notice that the progression produces root position dominant seventh chords a minor third apart on each downbeat. In **b.**, only these downbeat dominants are given, and you must fill in the intervening chords. In **c.**, only the bass is given.

c. Start the right hand in different positions and fill in the passing chords

17.10 Chopin: Nocturne, Op. 27, No. 2, 40–46

Chromatic passages such as this are difficult to read, to learn, and to memorize. But once we understand the harmonic patterns, our practicing becomes more efficient, and our appreciation of Chopin's genius deepens. As usual, start with the accompaniment, playing it with two hands in block chords. As you do this, notice as much as you can about the horizontal movement of the chromatic voice leading, and about the qualities and spellings of the vertical chords produced.

If we re-write the accompaniment as you just played it, in block chords with two hands, we can see the patterns more easily. An omnibus progression connects the opening V⁷ chord (spelled as a G#⁷) to the same chord at the end of the passage (now spelled as A♭⁷). There are two exceptions to the standard voice leading of the omnibus, creating diminished seventh chords, which are not normally part of this progression (play a standard omnibus on Chopin's bass line to find the differences). The harmonic rhythm speeds up as we approach the climax (shown by the changes of time signature in the reduction below). The reduction also suggests ways of re-naming some of the chords to make them easier to think (these enharmonic re-spellings are put in quotation marks). Play through this reduction twice, paying attention the first time to the horizontal movement of the individual voices, and naming the chords as pop symbols the second time. Once again, you'll probably find that you can play it from memory after that. We still have to learn the right-hand melody, of course, but it will make much more sense now that we understand its harmonic underpinning.

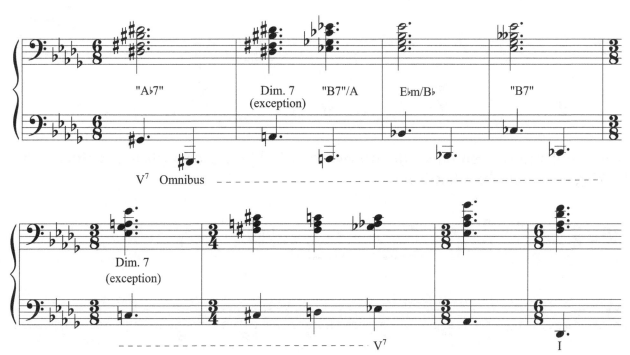

17.11 Beethoven: Piano Sonata in F, Op. 54, II, 33–45

In this passage, Beethoven uses an omnibus progression to modulate. Play the passage in block chords, describing the patterns and naming the chords as you play. As in the Chopin example, this omnibus also contains an exception to the standard pattern.

212 *Chromatic Voice Leading Techniques*

Now see if you can reproduce the passage, first in block chords, then as written, while looking only at the bass line below.

ENHARMONIC RE-SPELLING AND MODULATION

17.12 Beethoven: Piano Sonata in C Minor, Op. 13, I, 133–136

You have probably already noticed that certain chords—diminished sevenths and German augmented sixths in particular—can be spelled in different ways and yet sound the same when played on the piano. Composers sometimes exploit this enharmonic re-spelling, as it's called, to create a very special harmonic effect. When a chord is spelled and resolved first in one way, then re-spelled and resolved in a different way, it changes its identity and harmonic meaning. This effect is akin to that of the pivot chord, whose change of function only becomes apparent to us by what comes afterwards (see **9.3**).

In this passage, Beethoven uses an enharmonically re-spelled diminished seventh chord as a pivot chord to modulate from G minor to E minor (compare the two chords with asterisks). The effect is striking, and requires close listening and an emotional response from the player.

Linger and Listen: In the second half of measure 135, pause first on the B♮ in the left hand, then on the resolution to E minor in the right hand to fully appreciate this surprising harmonic twist. Notice the return of the diminished seventh chord in the right hand of measure 136, now as part of a dominant ninth chord.

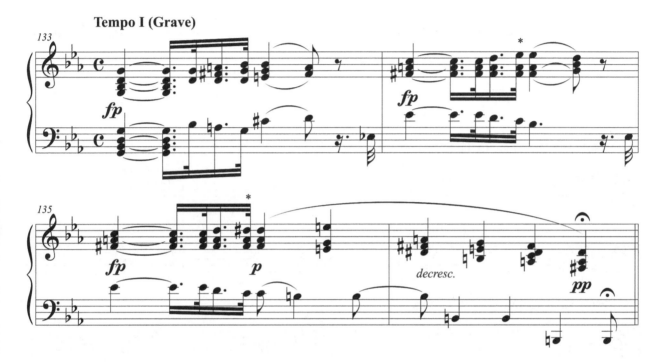

17.13 Enharmonic Re-Spelling of the Diminished Seventh Chord

Any diminished seventh chord can be spelled in four different ways, and thereby made to modulate to four different keys (normally minor keys, where vii°7 is diatonic, but it can also be borrowed in major keys). In the exercises below, the same diminished seventh chord is given four different spellings, making each of its four notes the leading tone to a different key. Play exercise **a.**, carefully studying the spellings of the diminished sevenths, their figured bass symbols, their resolutions, and the continuations to cadences in each of the four keys. Exercises **b.** and **c.** give only the starting chord, using the other two diminished seventh chords in the other two right-hand positions. Resolve them to the minor tonic indicated by the key signature, then improvise a continuation to a cadence.

b. Resolve and continue to the cadence.

c. Resolve and continue to the cadence.

17.14 Mozart: Adagio in B Minor, K. 540, 1–2 and 7–8

Compare these two phrases from the exposition of this somberly beautiful piece. In the second phrase, Mozart re-spells the secondary diminished chord from the first phrase to modulate from B minor to the relative major. On paper, the eye sees that the *sfp* chord in measure 7 is spelled with an F♮, but because of the B-minor context, the ear hears it as an E♯, making the succeeding E♮ and the consequent cadence in D major a highly expressive, and somehow soothing, turn of events.

Replace and Restore: Re-write measures 7–8 to stay in B minor, as the ear expects. You might employ the voice exchange idea that Mozart uses in measure 1, for example. When you restore the original, you should hear it with fresh ears.

17.15 Enharmonic Re-Spelling of the German Augmented Sixth Chord

On the piano, a chord spelled C-E-G-B♭ has the same sound as one spelled C-E-G-A♯, but its function is different. The first spelling is for the dominant of F, and the second for the German augmented sixth in E. This enharmonic re-spelling can therefore be used to modulate to (or merely tonicize) keys a half step apart. The two progressions below illustrate this phenomenon. As you play them, notice how the chords under the dotted brackets are re-spelled to change their function and tonal direction. Transpose to other keys and improvise similar progressions of your own.

17.16 Mendelssohn: Song Without Words, Op. 19, No. 5, 46–58

At the climax of this passage, Mendelssohn hammers out two German augmented sixth chords and their resolutions (measures 50–51), then re-spells the same chord as a dominant seventh, leading the music in a surprising new direction. Make a harmonic reduction (played, written, or both) of this entire passage, which contains patterns that you will recognize from previous chapters. Speak a narrative description of your reduction as you play it.

REPERTOIRE STUDY

17.17 Grieg: Lyric Piece, Op. 12, No. 4 ("Fairy Dance"), 1–32

Reduction: Play a block-chord reduction to find the basic progressions and patterns.
Analysis: Look for voice exchanges, key changes, an enharmonic re-spelling, the unusual resolution of the diminished seventh, and an augmented sixth chord. Name these patterns and chords as you play the reduction.

17.18 Chopin: Polonaise in C Minor, Op. 40, No. 2, 56–70

Reduction: In measures 56–58, reduce the harmony to a quarter-note rhythm. At the *pp* passage starting in measure 58, hold the chords for their full duration instead of repeating them as written. Mentally re-spell any chords that are difficult to read as written.

218 *Chromatic Voice Leading Techniques*

Analysis: Look for neighboring diminished seventh chords, chromatic voice exchanges, enharmonic re-spellings and modulations, and irregular resolutions. Narrate these findings as you play the reduction.

Expression: Consider how these harmonic surprises influence your use of *rubato* and dynamic shading.

Index

Bach, Johann Christoph Friedrich
  Solfeggio in D 105–6
Bach, Johann Sebastian
  Chaconne in D Minor 128
  English Suite No. 3 in G Minor, Prelude 136–8
  French Suites
    No. 2 in C Minor, Minuet 31
    No. 3 in B Minor, Minuet 32–3; Sarabande 58
    No. 5 in G Major, Gavotte 116–17
  Little Preludes
    in F, BWV 927 57–8
    in D, BWV 925 39
  Organ Sonata No. 4, Adagio 184
  Partita No. 5 in G, Prelude 142
  Prelude in G, BWV 902 64
  Well-Tempered Clavier, Book 1
    Prelude in C 121–3
    Prelude in C♯ Minor 143
    Prelude in B♭ 35–7
Beethoven, Ludwig van
  Bagatelle, Op. 33, No. 4 195–6
  Piano Concertos
    No. 4, Op. 58, I 20–1, II 96, III 166
    No. 5, Op. 73, II 41
  Piano Sonatas
    in F Minor, Op. 2, No. 1, II 66; IV 66
    in E♭, Op. 7, III 108–9
    in C Minor, Op. 10, No. 1, I 152–3; II 84
    in D, Op. 10, No. 3, II 157
    in C Minor, Op. 13, I, 171–2, 212–13; II 97–8
    in E♭, Op. 27, No. 1, III 84
    in C♯ Minor, Op. 27, No. 2, I 184
    in D, Op. 28, II 25
    in E♭, Op. 31, No. 3, II 85
    in F, Op. 54, II 211–12
    in E, Op. 109, I 42
  Rondo in C, Op. 51, No. 1 90–1
  Variations on the Russian Dance from *Das Waldmädchen*, WoO 71 165–6
Brahms, Johannes
  Ich schell mein Horn ins Jammertal, Op. 43, No. 3 12–13
  Romanze, Op. 118, No. 5 42–3

cadence feel 109–10, 117
cadences: deceptive 16–17, with first inversion triads 28–9, with root positions triads 15–16
Chopin, Frederic
  Ballade No. 1, Op. 23 130–1, 150–1
  Etudes, Op. 10
    No. 3 197
    No. 4 158
    No. 6 187–8
  Impromptu No. 1, Op. 29 197–8
  Mazurkas
    Op. 6, No. 4 100
    Op. 63, No. 3 196
    Op. 67, No. 4 206
  Nocturnes
    Op. 15, No. 3 12
    Op. 27, No. 2 210–11
    Op. 37, No. 1 12
  Polonaise, Op. 40, No. 2 217–18
  Waltzes
    Op. 34, No. 2 159–60
    Op. 69, No. 2 91–2
chorale style 126
chord position 5
chromatic neighbor chords 205–8
complete dominant seventh chord 73–4
continuo accompaniment 30–3
Couperin, François
  Les Coucous bénévoles, Pièces de Clavecin, Ordre XIII 128–9

dissonance, treatment of 48, 50–1, 123
doubling: in deceptive cadences 16, in first inversion triads 27–8, in Neapolitan sixth chords 183

enharmonic respelling 212–13; of augmented sixth chords 215–16; of diminished seventh chords 213–15

Grieg, Edvard
  Lyric Pieces
    Op. 12, No. 3 "The Watchman's Song" 132
    Op. 12, No. 4 "Fairy Dance" 217
    Op. 43, No. 1 "Butterfly" 180–1, 188–90
  Norwegian Folk Tunes, Op. 66, No. 18 "I Wander Deep in Thought" 134–5

Handel, George Frideric
  Lessons for Princess Anne 13–14, 29–30, 141
Haydn, Franz Joseph
  Piano Sonatas
    in G Hob. XVI:8, II 111–12
    in A, Hob. XVI:12, II 40
    in E Minor, Hob. XVI:34, I 155–6; III 114–15
    in C, Hob. XVI:35, III 23
    in A♭, Hob. XVI:46, I 22, 40–1; II 50, 56
Highlight and Hear (practice method) 100

incomplete dominant seventh 73–5

keyboard style 5, 74
Kuhnau, Johann
  Prelude in G 149–50

Leo, Leonardo
  Toccata in G Minor 33–4
Linger and Listen (practice method) 50
Liszt, Franz
  Au lac de Wallenstadt, Années de pèlerinage (première année), 206–7
  Funérailles, Harmonies poétiques et religieuses, No. 7 204–5
  Pater noster, Harmonies poétiques et religieuses, No. 5 4

melody and accompaniment style 5, 68, 86
Mendelssohn, Felix
  Songs Without Words
    Op. 19, No. 1 133–4
    Op. 19, No. 5 216
    Op. 85, No. 3 67
    Op. 102, No. 4 185
  Variations, Op. 82 179–80
Mozart, Wolfgang Amadeus
  Adagio in B Minor, K. 540 214–15
  Fantasy in D Minor, K. 397 86
  Piano Concertos
    in D minor, K. 466, I 52–3; III 156
    in A, K. 488, II 182
    in C, K. 503, III 129–30, 143–4
  Piano Sonatas
    in B♭, K. 281, III 23–4
    in D, K. 284, III 112–13, 191–2
    in A Minor, K. 310, III 24
    in D, K. 311, II 65–6, 165; III 93–4
    in C, K. 330, II 60, 64–5, 110–11
    in A, K. 331, I 51
    in F, K. 332, II 51–2
    in B♭, K. 333, I 46–7, 50
  Variations on Ah, vous dirai-je Maman, K. 265 56–7

narration, analytical 169

omnibus progression 208–12
outer voice reduction 22
overtones 64

parallel sixths 21
pivot chords 110–11
pop symbols 205
Prepare and Resolve (practice method) 50–1

Rachmaninoff, Serge
  Nocturne, Op. 10, No. 1 202–3
Repeat and React (practice method) 50
Replace and Restore (practice method) 129

Schubert, Franz
  German Dances
    D. 420, No. 12 101
    D. 783, No. 15 115–16
  Impromptus
    in E♭, D. 899, No. 2 130, 144
    in A♭, D. 935, No. 2 80–1
    in B♭, D. 935, No. 3 172–3
  Ländler, D. 734, No. 12 88
  Moments musicaux, D. 780
    No. 4 157
    No. 6 176–7
  Piano Sonatas
    in A Minor, D. 845, I 7, 208–9; II 174
    in B♭, D. 960, IV 7–8
  Valse sentimentale, D. 779, No. 18 72–3
Schumann, Robert
  Album for the Young, Op. 68
    No. 20 162–3
    No. 28, Erinnerung 113–14
    No. 30 131–2
    No. 40, Nordisches Lied 26
  Arabesque, Op. 18 106–7
  Carnaval, Op. 9, Chiarina 160–1
  Kinderszenen, Op. 15
    No. 13, Der Dichter spricht 177
  Kreisleriana, Op. 16, No. 7 145
  Romanze, Op. 28, No. 1 100–1
  Waltz, Albumblätter, Op. 124, No. 4 42
sequences: types of 37–8; with diatonic seventh chords 138–40; with secondary diminished chords 164; with secondary dominant chords 97–9; with suspensions 54–5; with triads 37–8
spread position accompaniment 72, 74–5, 88

Tchaikovsky, Pyotr Ilyich
  January (The Seasons) 65
tension and release 9
transposition: analytical 95–9; with clef substitution 128, 155

voice exchange 21; double 61
voice leading: of diminished seventh chords 153–4; of dominant seventh chords 73; of root position triads 6; of secondary dominant chords 94; of sequences with seventh chords 138; of supertonic seventh chords 123